The Proper Care of
BURMESE CATS

DENNIS KELSEY-WOOD

Dedication

Dedicated to Ralph. He owns
Dr. Judith Topilow. She's a great
baby doctor...and a greater
human being.

Distributed in the UNITED STATES by T.F.H. Publications, Inc., One T.F.H.
Plaza, Neptune City, NJ 07753; in CANADA to the Pet Trade by H & L Pet
Supplies Inc., 27 Kingston Crescent, Kitchener, Ontario N2B 2T6; Rolf C.
Hagen Ltd., 3225 Sartelon Street, Montreal 382 Quebec; in CANADA to the
Book Trade by Macmillan of Canada (A Division of Canada Publishing
Corporation), 164 Commander Boulevard, Agincourt, Ontario M1S 3C7; in
ENGLAND by T.F.H. Publications, PO Box 15, Waterlooville PO7 6BQ; in
AUSTRALIA AND THE SOUTH PACIFIC by T.F.H. (Australia) Pty. Ltd.,
Box 149, Brookvale 2100 N.S.W., Australia; in NEW ZEALAND by Ross
Haines & Son, Ltd., 82 D Elizabeth Knox Place, Panmure, Auckland, New
Zealand; in the PHILIPPINES by Bio-Research, 5 Lippay Street, San
Lorenzo Village, Makati, Rizal; in SOUTH AFRICA by Multipet Pty. Ltd.,
P.O. Box 35347, Northway, 4065, South Africa. Published by T.F.H.
Publications, Inc. Manufactured in the United States of America by T.F.H.
Publications, Inc.

CONTENTS

THE PROPER CARE OF BURMESE CATS

Photo credits: Creative Photographers, Isabelle Français, Kenneth T. Nemuras, Robert Pearcy, Fritz Prenzel, Purina, Inc., Mrs. L.D. Sample, Vince Serbin, Skotzke & Lucas, Sally Anne Thompson, Tetsu Yamazaki.

Drawings: John R. Quinn.

Introduction

Exactly when the modern felids appeared in a form we recognize today as being cats is not known, nor is it ever likely to be for the following two basic reasons. Firstly, the earliest felids were forest dwellers, and such habitats are not conducive to good fossilization, so the fossil record of cats is rather patchy and inconclusive. Secondly, and a point often oversimplified in popular literature, is that all animal life is a continuum species. The meaning of this is that each present-day species has evolved from other species over millions of years.

This statement implies that changes—thus new species—happen relatively quickly and are identifiable within a short time period. This is not the case. Herein lies one of the major problems when discussing evolution, because while we can separate animals into obvious, distinct species within any one time period, it is not possible to differentiate species along a time axis. To say one species has developed from another is true only insofar as scientists apply species labels to animals in different time periods. It must be remembered that the cat has always been a cat, but if you went far enough back, generation by generation, you would slowly meet ancestors that also became dogs or skunks or weasels; it would therefore be difficult to pinpoint any single point in time when you could say "this is not a cat" based on the criteria you were using at that point—rather than by today's concept of a cat.

Given this aspect, and appreciating it, it can then be said that the modern idea of a cat has existed

Burmese have grown in popularity as more and more people have discovered the many wonderful qualities of the breed. They have won a large number of fanciers, who love these cats both as pets and as show animals. This pair is owned by Herb Zwecker.

for no more than about seven million years. Its precursors were carnivores which exhibited features which are as typically dog, bear, civet or weasel-like as they are cat-like. Prior to this time there were a number of very large saber-toothed cats to be found around the world, but these have no relationship to the modern cats, only insofar as all mammals share common ancestry in the mists of time. The saber-tooths occupied the top of the predatory chain for millions of years until they were displaced by the modern roaring cats such as lions and tigers.

The latter developed superior killing techniques and were faster; they could catch the much quicker ungulates that had evolved which the saber-tooths, being slower, could not prey on. The last of the great dagger-toothed cats vanished forever about 15,000 years ago. It is known that most, if not all, present-day cat species were in evidence about one million years ago, and it is generally thought that they are of Old World origins, though this is by no means a firmly established fact.

DOMESTICATION

As with the evolution of the cat, it is not known when felines first took up an association with humans. The dog was domesticated by about 10,000 years ago but the cat probably only started to enter human settlements about 4000 years ago, possibly as a result of kittens being captured or found and then reared, almost as pets, much as they are today. It may have been noticed how good they were at killing rodents, thus they would have been welcomed in settlements where grain stores were kept.

Certainly the Egyptians considered cats to be very important, and households had statues and carvings of their favorite pets. Indeed, a complete cult became established around the cat, which was believed to have mystical powers.

The domestication of cats commenced some 4,000 years ago. They became prized pets because of their abilities as ratters. Additionally, many people believed that cats were endowed with mystical powers.

When pets died, they were mummified with the same sense of occasion as befitted humans, and mice were also mummified in order to provide food for the cats on their journey to the afterworld. The god of war in ancient Egypt was called Sekmet, and appeared as a lion; his smaller relation was Bastet, or Pascht, the cat-headed woman god. The great sun god was Ra and was worshipped in the form of the cat. Each day Ra would slay the god of darkness, so it can be appreciated how important the Egyptians regarded the cat. To injure or kill a cat was punishable by death.

The Chinese were also a nation which held the cat in great esteem, and it is thought that domestication of cats in the Far East came somewhat later than in Egypt—possibly about 1000 BC. Again, the Far Eastern peoples believed cats had great powers, and it was also thought that people's souls, after death, entered the body of a cat—so felines were given great respect.

The color of the Birman cat is thought to have been given to it by the goddess Tsun-Kyan-Kse following the death of a devoted priest, and this is but one of the many legends that associate cats with many Eastern religions.

The Romans regarded the cat as a symbol of liberty, and as their armies marched all-conquering throughout

The Burmese shares its popularity in the cat cult with other felines, including this cat: the Birman. Some believe the color of the Birman was given to the cat by a goddess. Owner, Betty A. Cowles.

the Near East and Europe, so in their wake was the cat taken with families who settled in the different lands. For many years the cat enjoyed both privilege and status as the important killer of rats and mice, which were the scourge of all early peoples who stored the grain harvested from their toil in the field. However, this changed during the Middle Ages, when cats came to be associated with witchcraft and, as a result, were killed by burning, hanging and drowning as well as by other terrible means. Not all cats were so treated, but any that entered certain homes were; those on farms were left to continue their work as destroyers of vermin. Black cats are traditionally bringers of good luck, but in the Middle Ages it wasn't such a lucky color for the cats, as these were thought to be the most sinister of all. Happily, things got better in Europe, and the cat once again became a popular pet—helped along both by the many members of royalty who owned them, and by famous poets, writers and artists who did likewise. The prophet Mohammed was very much a lover of cats, and it is said it was he who gave his own pet—and all other cats into perpetuity—the ability to always land on its feet when it fell from a height. The statesman Winston Churchill left a sum of money in his will in order that cats should always be kept in his country home.

He was not alone in this, as the infamous Cardinal Richelieu also left money in order that his large family of cats should be well provided for.

By the turn of the 20th century not only were cats very firmly established as household pets, but by then there was a growing interest in developing new breeds and trying to establish foreign breeds. The cat fancy as such was thus beginning. Until this century, only a few breeds were recognized, but during the last half-century cats have really taken off and breeds have proliferated considerably. The names can be a bit misleading at times, since it has become accepted that a country name can be given to a breed that may well have been developed elsewhere—the Burmese is a case in point. However, whatever the name of the breed, there is no questioning as to how popular cats have now become. They have many advantages for a family since they do not take up a lot of room; they are quiet, extremely clean in their habits, and they retain an air of independence. They do not have to be taken for a walk, as they will happily exercise themselves if given the freedom to do so. Feeding cats is simple and not costly. In the case of the Burmese, there is a bonus because this breed exhibits many characteristics that are almost dog-like, so you have the best of both worlds!

In the following

chapters we will look at all the subjects that the interested owner is likely to need to know about—history, selection, feeding, breeding and much more, so that owners will have a complete and concise reference to consult. One thing is for sure—you have made the right decision in the choice of cat breed, because the Burmese is in every way a truly delightful cat to have as a companion and is indeed a peer among the many other cats from which you may have chosen.

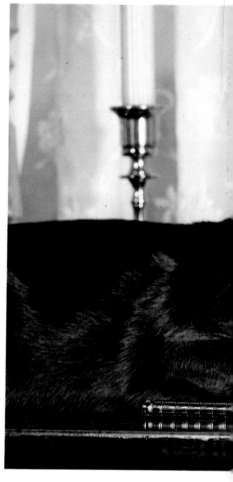

For the person who wants an aristocratic yet companionable cat, the Burmese is the ideal choice. Its keen intelligence and even disposition make it a joy to own.

Burmese and Birman kittens settling down for a nap. Their close body contact serves as a substitute for the warmth and security of their mothers.

Feline Characteristics

To fully understand and appreciate cats, it is necessary to know a little about their place in the world and what makes them cats. As a group, they are very easily identified and not to be confused with other animal species; yet if you were to try to define a cat in brief terms you would find this all but impossible. Most of their features are found in other animals, especially in carnivores, so it is only in the degree of modification to a basic overall structure that makes them felids.

Many millions of years ago the early carnivores started to diversify, each adapting to take its place in a world that was forever changing. Some stayed within dense forest, some moved onto open grasslands and others to aquatic areas. In each case this meant modifications in order to take advantage of the habitat in which it lived. The most important modification of all is probably in the dentition, and this is because the ability to cope with a given type of food is fundamental to the rest of the animal's development in terms of its shape. It is thus within the structure of the teeth that a cat is most easily differentiated from other carnivores.

A felid's teeth are highly specialized tools, and their single primary function is to kill other animals. This they achieve either by dislocation of the vertebrae at the base of the skull, or by a throat bite which causes suffocation. Other carnivores, such as mongooses and stoats, also use this technique. However, on becoming highly specialized, there is usually a price to pay somewhere along the line and, in the case of cats, they are less able to cope

Since domesticated cats do not have to kill for their food, as do their brothers in the wild, their teeth are not completely utilized the way nature intended.

with bone and vegetable matter than other carnivores—such as bears, or dogs. A cat cannot chew very well, which is why you will see your cat cope with meat by turning its head sideways to shear meat from bone and then swallow it. Meat is easily digested compared with plant cellulose. This means that a cat which has a relatively simple digestive system, can digest meat more easily than it can digest vegetable matter. Thus it can be seen how the cat has opted to become a prime predator. A dog is also a major predator but has developed so that it can also get by in hard times on plant matter and carrion, like bone left by other carnivores. This means its teeth cannot be as specialized as those of cats, and in turn this affects many other aspects of its life and construction.

The cat's incisors are very small, while the canine teeth are much enlarged to effect lethal bites. The carnassial teeth (last premolar in the upper jaw and first molar in the lower) are large and pointed so they can shear meat. The cat has just four molars, compared with a dog's ten. This fact enables a dog to grind food such as bone and even cereal.

While a cow, goat or horse has no problems in overcoming its diet (plants not being noted for moving around), the same is not so for a carnivore, as its basic diet is unlikely to stand still to

You can tell that this Burmese has recently given birth by the prominence of her nipples. Her milk will fully provide her kittens with the nutrition they need in the early weeks of life.

be eaten. This means that, apart from actually killing its prey, it must first get to it, and again carnivores have chosen to develop two basic methods of achieving this. In cats and dogs we can see this exemplified at its best. A dog is a tireless runner, so it can pursue its prey over vast distances. If it loses sight of it, this does not matter, since its powers of scent are amazing—it will simply follow the trail. A cat has no ability to maintain a chase; it is a sprinter par excellence and its entire body is built for just this purpose. If its prey eludes that burst of speed from the cat, then the cat will simply have a rest and then look for another potential meal. Thus cats are also extremely good at laying around, it being quite natural to them!

We often regard cats as being "laid back" or even lazy at times, but actually it is important that a cat rest a great deal in order to build up the energy and muscle needed for explosive bursts of action. Conversely, the reverse is true in dogs, which will play for hours because they are endurance animals, so much playing is a natural way of keeping trim.

You will find that your Burmese reflects in the things it does its natural wild instincts, which are never far below the apparent veneer of domestication. These instincts are very strong indeed, and, once your pet is out in the garden, it is as much a prime predator in its little world as the tiger or leopard is in the wild. Indeed, in most ways, the domestic cat is the classic example of a felid.

BODY

Generally, felids have a body shape that will fit into a rectangle, which means the length is greater than the height. Thus the legs are short, relative to body length; this is a useful adaptation in a carnivore that needs to approach its prey unseen until the very last possible moment. Such a build means cats can crouch low to the ground, and the great suppleness of the limbs is such that,

A lilac Burmese kitten. Even at this young age, it exhibits the litheness and suppleness characteristic of felines.

in this position, the cat can also move forward. No other animal can do this as well as a cat. The muscles of the hind legs are very strong, most important both for unleashing instant bursts of speed and for springing onto small rodents from a distance—or leaping into a tree. With the exception of the big cats, such as lions and tigers, most cats are excellent climbers and, when not actually hunting, are happier when laying above ground level. This is not only a protective device to save them from predators larger than themselves, but also acts as a good vantage point for seeing potential prey species in undergrowth or moving among rocks.

While cats are superb at climbing up trees, they are less talented at getting down! Their sharp claws give them the former ability but are totally the wrong shape for effecting the reverse; added to this is the fact that the body weight of cats is somewhat heavier towards the back end. Such a configuration is thus fine going up but less beneficial coming down, which is why cats descend in a rather less than dignified fashion by descending backwards, using their front claws to grip while lowering themselves as best they can until they reach a height from which they can suddenly turn around and leap to the ground. This is the reason cats get themselves in all sorts of trouble! One of our Burmese had the skill to climb up the vertical house wall made of pebbledash in order to gain entry to a bedroom window. However, if the window was closed, he then had a problem—and sometimes a long wait if we were out! Such are cats.

It is important that a cat be able to sheath its claws since they are so vital to its mode of life. They must always be sharp in order to maintain a good hold on mice, rats or whatever—and to use as defensive weapons against other cats or dogs. If, like dogs, they were not sheathed, then they would wear out and be

Cats spend a good deal of time of sitting quietly or sleeping. Some people associate this behavior with laziness, but that is not the case. Periods of rest enable the cat to maintain the energy it needs for its sudden bursts of activity.

less than efficient as a result. The cheetah is unique among cats in that it cannot sheath its claws—one of numerous adaptations in this species which make it the world's fastest animal. I should mention that one of the very worst things you can do to a cat is to have it declawed; this terrible practice is illegal in the UK and in numerous states of the USA, but not globally. There is not a single merit to such a practice, because the cat is thus denied its most basic weapon of defense which enables it to escape attackers by climbing to a safe refuge. Any persons who do it in order to save the furniture from being scratched would be better advised to not keep any animals whatsoever, as clearly they are more concerned with material objects than with living creatures.

The tail of a cat is usually long and may be well furred or, as in the case of Burmese, with only a short covering of hair—thus reflecting the climate in which the cat originally lived. The tail is a balancing aid to cats both when in trees, where it acts like a tightrope walker's pole to shift the center of gravity to compensate for any over-balance, and when running at speed in order to correct balance as the cat changes direction. It is, of course, also used as a social indicator of the cat's mood. Unlike a dog, when a cat flicks its tail, it is generally a sign that it is annoyed, or at least disturbed, about something.

The head shape in all cats is basically round, and this is linked to its carnivorous lifestyle. Because the canine teeth are extremely large, it follows that a cat must be able to open its mouth quite wide in order to bring its teeth to bear on

Facing page: A cat and a dog can be good friends and companions for each other, if they are properly introduced. Naturally, you should remain close by when the two make their acquaintance.

the neck of its prey. A round shape is more conducive to this and also permits a shorter distance between the canine teeth and the muscles of the head and neck. This allows for the maximum amount of pressure to be applied into the bite, which is so crucial to a cat. A cat will tend to bite and hang on in order to drive in its canine teeth, whereas a dog is more inclined to bite in order to shake its victim or merely to hang on, pending the arrival of other dogs to aid in overcoming larger prey species. The contrasting characteristics of dogs and cats serve to illustrate why cats cannot be treated like dogs, and why each reacts the way it does to given situations which always reflect the wild inclinations and mode of living.

SENSES

The senses of any carnivore are necessarily keen because this is important in seeking their prey. Eyesight in cats is excellent and about on a par with that of man in being able to focus at distant objects; dogs are less able to do this and rely on an image coupled with scenting the air. In terms of the field of vision, the cat has about 285°, the dog a little over 290° (depending on the breed, however) and man has about 210°. When cross-over or binocular vision is considered, then the cat has 130° compared to man's 120° and the dog's 110°.

The ability to see well at

For purposes of comparison, the text in this section is accompanied by illustrations of other breeds of cat. Shown above—Eyes: Oriental Shorthair, silver mackerel tabby; Norwegian Forest Cat, brown classic tabby and white; Russian Blue. Note: On this page and the succeeding pages depicting eye studies, the caption identifications are given top to bottom.

Eyes: Himalayan, seal point; Norwegian Forest Cat, blue mackerel tabby; Persian, red.

Since 1952, *Tropical Fish Hobbyist* has been the source of accurate, up-to-the-minute, and fascinating information on every facet of the aquarium hobby. Join the more than 50,000 devoted readers worldwide who wouldn't miss a single issue.

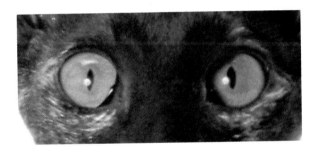

Eyes: Persian, shaded silver; Oriental Shorthair, tortoiseshell; Manx, odd-eyed white.

night requires that the eyes have many rods in the retina, which all carnivores have; additionally, most carnivores have an extra tissue layer, known as the tapetum lucidum, which effectively reflects light back into the eye in order to trigger off receptors it failed to do when first entering the eye. The result is that a cat can see about six times better than we can in the dark. No animal can see in total darkness, but what appears to us as "total" may indeed still contain some light, and it is this that night-hunters are able to utilize. To a cat, an almost black night to a human would appear like a very overcast day by comparison.

However, in order to see well during the day, the cat must close its pupil almost totally to shut out the light from its very sensitive retina. It is the reflective layer in the eye that gives most night animals the well-known nightshine when light is shone onto them by a flashlight or other means.

The cat, along with most other carnivores studied, has the ability to distinguish colors, but the cat gives no particular importance to such, which is why it was thought for many years that cats were colorblind; very special training techniques were required to persuade the cat to display its ability; the dog also attaches no importance to colors, though I suspect they use them somewhat more than do cats.

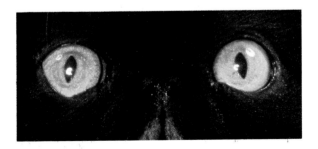

Eyes: Scottish Fold, tortoiseshell and white; Norwegian Forest Cat, brown mackerel tabby and white; Persian, black.

The sense of hearing in cats is very marked, which is not surprising since cats must be capable of picking up the faintest high-pitched squeak of rodents. The cat can hear sounds very much out of a human's capability and, perhaps surprisingly, can even hear sounds of a higher frequency than can a dog, which is traditionally regarded as having super hearing. It is this ability that might give rise to a cat and dog's sixth sense of foretelling disaster; they can pick up sound waves well before we humans hear them and so can exhibit anxiety when all appears normal to us. In spite of this superb hearing, you will find your Burmese can be remarkably deaf when it so chooses!

The cat's sense of smell is not its most outstanding ability but, even so, it is considerably better than ours. Smell is not especially important to humans, so organizing worthwhile tests to establish thresholds in animals is difficult and, other than in the dog, little work has been done with carnivores— including the cat, which otherwise is one of the most studied flesh-eaters. Animals use scent in many ways; firstly they track prey to a greater or lesser degree by it, and it plays an especially important part in their social structure and reproductive habits. The cat's great affinity for catnip may well be because within this plant's odor there is a

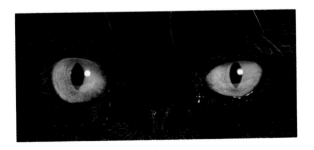

Eyes: Persian, tortoiseshell; Persian, red; Persian, black.

chemical which is almost comparable to the scent a female in estrus gives out. You will notice when your cat goes to eat its dinner that it carefully sniffs it first; this tells it far more about what is on offer than we humans can begin to imagine. Beyond not liking the look of a medicinal pill, a cat can tell by its smell that it isn't something it will enjoy; thus all pills will normally be left nicely in the bottom of a bowl of food into which you took great pains to disguise it! You can't smell the pill, but it probably smells awful to the cat—a fact the producers possibly do not take too much into account.

As far as taste goes, cats are rather persnickety and are rather less willing to take non-meats than are dogs, who, being more opportune feeders, will generally take anything that resembles food. Again, this reflects the differing ways each feeds in the wild state, and cats are very much prime carnivores and very much secondary vegetarians— though hungry cats will eat whatever is on offer— but this is not the best way to establish normal feeding habits. In the wild the cat will obtain its vegetable needs from the partly digested foods within the stomachs of the animals it kills.

Cats have no taste buds for sweet items and, generally, will ignore cookies, chocolate, and similar items. However, some cats do develop a sweet tooth, and among

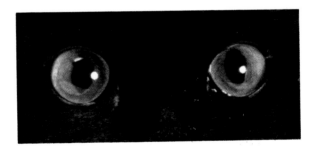

Eyes: Persian, red classic tabby; Siamese, blue lynx point; Norwegian Forest Cat, black.

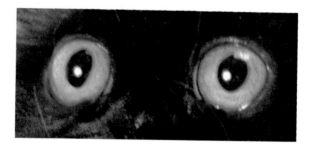

Eyes: Persian, red; Persian, blue smoke; Persian, cream and white.

our own collection is one that will eat anything from jam to bits of fruit, and another which will take chocolate and cookies. I hasten to add that these things have no benefits to cats and are not recommended, but even people who should know better often indulge their pets with forbidden fruits. Maybe it would sound better if I said we only indulge them in the interests of scientific research!

It was thought that sweet items caused digestive upsets, but this is not so, or it is a case that reaction to sweet items is a matter of individual consideration. There is good reason to believe that the eating habits of cats is changing with domestication and more in keeping with what such cats actually are receiving these days. Certain breeds may well be more predisposed to accept less meat in their diets than will others that are from less domesticated lineage. It is certainly true that eating habits are acquired very early in life, so that cats fed on correct diets are unlikely to ever eat sweet items later in life, our two sweet-toothed cats certainly not being typical of the cats we have owned over the years.

DEXTERITY

Cats have very supple bodies and are able to get themselves into all sorts of trouble by squeezing through openings they shouldn't—like open washing machine doors, cupboards, grille openings, etc. This ability is natural; wild cats must be able to move through branches or undergrowth in such a way as not to disturb loose stones, break branches, or even cause the latter to make a noise which would immediately alert their prey. The whiskers of a cat are sense receptors and give the cat instant warning if its body is likely to touch a branch by which it is creeping. It is also thought that certain hairs on the cat's body also have sensory tips that tell the cat that it is brushing against an object.

The forelimbs of cats are also quite useful in that they can use them rather like hands and can rotate the paws in a way a dog cannot. However, they are not especially well adapted among carnivores in limb movements—animals such as raccoons and otters are more able to use their paws to handle items. Nonetheless, cats do rely a great deal on using their paws to "test" things, as you will notice, and they are very quick in such reactions. However, the forelimbs are essentially tools for grasping and holding objects, whether this be a ball of wool or a mouse.

HUNTING INSTINCT

The cat's threshold for endurance in stalking is extremely low, but this is an obvious need in a carnivore that relies on stealth to approach its prey. A cat must be prepared to stalk the instant it sees anything

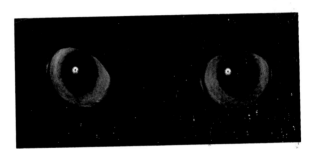

Eyes: Persian, chinchilla silver; Ragdoll, seal point, Singapura.

that resembles food, for only occasionally will a stalk result in an attack, and even more rarely will an attack result in a kill. The cat that does not stalk too often becomes a very hungry cat, but of course in the comparative luxury of your home the food is provided. Therefore, you see the instinct showing up as your pet stalks your dog, or its fellow cats or a piece of string. The urge is so strong that the cat cannot resist the opportunity to follow its natural ways. You will notice how, just before it attacks, its backside wobbles from side to side as it treads the floor with its back feet. Exactly why cats do this is not known for sure, but having studied hundreds of cats during this action, I have come to believe the cat makes very minor corrections in its foot positions and also assesses the firmness and angle of the ground beneath each rear foot so that it can adjust the pressure in order to obtain maximum thrust without the risk of either foot slipping—which could make the difference between a kill and a near-miss (of which there will be a great number anyway). It is akin to a sprinter as he readies himself to leap from his starting block at maximum speed.

Whenever you sit watching your Burmese, it is interesting to ponder its actions and characteristics and think how they relate to its life in the wild.

The Breed Standard

While the origins of many cat breeds are obscure and lost in the mists of time, this is not so with the Burmese, which can be traced back to the cat from which the breed was to be developed. This cat was called Wong Mau and was exported from Burma to the USA by Dr. Joseph Thompson in 1930.

Wong Mau was a small female of Siamese type, but of a brown coloration that differed somewhat from that seen in typical Siamese of the period. She was obviously a mutant color form of the Siamese type of cat that is very common to that part of Asia. However, in the 1930s, little was known about cat genetics, so most breeding was conducted in a pioneering sort of manner. Fortunately, Dr. Thompson perceived he had a somewhat special cat, so he persuaded Dr. Clyde Keeler and a geneticist, Billie Gerst, to assist him in a series of breedings involving his brown female and Siamese. The object was to establish the genotype of Wong Mau. Initial results were not impressive, and it was thought the kittens were merely rather poor examples of Siamese. However, breeding continued, and by careful selection and backcrossing, the Burmese was eventually established as a pure-breeding cat. The results of these breedings were presented as a paper which was published in the *American Journal of Heredity* in 1943.

During the course of its development, the Burmese has changed in appearance, which is reflected by comparison of the present-day standard to that which was in use during the 1950s. Present-day Burmese are somewhat heavier than the originals and also have a more

Body studies: a chocolate Burmese and an American Shorthair, silver classic tabby. Note: On this page and the succeeding pages of body studies, the caption identifications are given top to bottom.

Body study of a Burmese. Members of this breed are medium sized and compact in appearance.

rounded face. The effect of this latter aspect is to give the ears the appearance of being somewhat smaller, though in reality this is not so. Generally, Burmese in the USA are less obviously of Siamese origins than are those seen in the UK. Australia's first Burmese was in fact imported from the UK, so development in that country was based along British bloodlines, and was a recent development since the original import to Australia, named Tomahawk, arrived on their shores in 1957.

There is sometimes an implication that present-day Burmese are the result of crossing Burmese with Siamese, and this does tend to be misleading because it suggests that there was already in existence a breed of cat known as the Burmese. This is not so; Wong Mau was undoubtedly a cat of mixed heritage but was of a "type" we call foreign or Siamese. Her singular asset was that she carried the gene now identified as *cb*, which is a gene that effectively dilutes black color to brown. We also know that the Siamese pattern is in the same series of mutations and is just one below the Burmese gene in its ability to show itself.

The Burmese was much appreciated in the USA after it became established and was given recognition by the Cat Fanciers' Association in 1936, only a few years after Wong

Mau's arrival on American shores. However, the CFA became dissatisfied with the way people were breeding the Burmese and withdrew registration for the breed in 1947. Things improved as a result, and in 1957 the breed was again allowed in the CFA register.

Today, Burmese are making considerable progress and have become extremely popular as exhibition cats, their nature being most conducive to this aspect of the cat fancy. As pets they really have everything going for them, as they are extremely affectionate, highly intelligent, and their short glossy coat needs only minimal attention. There is a good range of colors to choose from, so all in all their future success is both assured and predictable.

THE STANDARD OF THE BREED

One of the difficulties all writers on cats (and dogs) have is that relating to a given breed's standard of excellence. Books today are very international in their distribution—sadly, the same is not the case for official standards. This problem is made more difficult because in the USA and Australia there is not one overall governing body but a number—eight in the USA alone. Each of these associations issues its own standard and it is clearly not possible to reproduce each in a single book intended as a general guide to this breed. The situation in the UK differs insomuch as all feline matters are under the single control of the Governing Council of the Cat Fancy. I have therefore chosen to quote the British standard for the Burmese. It is essentially the same as that of other countries, but clearly any persons requiring more than just basic knowledge of the breed, that is, breeders and exhibitors, are advised to contact their own registration body and request the appropriate standard of that organization.

Whenever any group of people devises a system of classification, it is usually not without its peculiarities, and this is so in many of the smaller livestock groups—cats not being atypical of these. Within cats the word "breed" is used extremely loosely. What is essentially a breed is called a section and it is given a number. In the case of Burmese, this is 27, which is applied to the brown Burmese (sable in the USA). All other colors are then given letters of this number—27a is the blue variety, 27b the chocolate variety and so on. The reader, on seeing such a system, may be perplexed but is assured that a blue Burmese and a cream Burmese are one and the same breed, of which they are merely color variants.

THE STANDARD OF POINTS FOR BURMESE

The Burmese is an elegant cat of a foreign

Body studies: a Cornish Rex, parti-color, and a Devon Rex, white.

type, which is positive and quite individual to the breed. Any suggestion of either Siamese type, or the cobbiness of a British cat, must be regarded as a fault.

Body, legs and tail— The body should be of medium length and size, feeling hard and muscular, and heavier than its appearance indicates. The chest should be strong, and rounded in profile, the back straight from shoulder to rump. Legs should be slender and in proportion to the body; hind legs slightly longer than front; paws neat and oval in shape. The tail should be straight and of medium length, not heavy at base, and tapering only slightly to a rounded tip without bone defect. A visible kink or other bone defect in the tail is a fault, precluding the award of challenge certificate, but an invisible defect at the extreme tip may be overlooked in an otherwise excellent specimen.

Head, ears and eyeset—The head should be slightly rounded on top, with good breadth between the ears, having wide cheek bones and tapering to a short blunt wedge. The jaw should be wide at the hinge and the chin firm. A muzzle pinch is a bad fault. Ears should be medium in size, set well apart on the skull, broad at the base, with slightly rounded tips, the outer line of the ears continuing the shape of the upper part of the face. This may not be possible

Body studies: an American Curl, seal lynx point, and an American Shorthair, red classic tabby.

in mature males who develop a fullness of cheek. In profile the ears should be seen to have a slight forward tilt. There should be a distinct nose break, and in profile the chin should show a strong lower jaw. The eyes,

Eye colour—Eyes should be any shade of yellow from chartreuse to amber, with golden yellow preferred. Green eyes are a serious fault in Brown Burmese, but Blue Burmese may show a slight fading of colour.

Eyes: Scottish Fold, blue mackerel.

which should be set well apart, should be large and lustrous, the top line of the eye showing a straight oriental slant towards the nose, the lower line being rounded. Either round or oriental eyes are a fault.

Green eyes with more blue than yellow pigmentation must preclude the award of challenge certificate in Burmese of all colours.

Coat—The coat should be short, fine, satin-like in

texture, lying close to the body. The glossy coat is a distinctive feature of Burmese, and is indicative of good health.

Condition—Cats should be well-muscled, with good weight for size, lively and alert.

tabby barring and, overall, a lighter colour than adults. The presence of a few white hairs may be overlooked in an otherwise excellent cat, but a noticeable number of white hairs, or a white patch, is a serious fault

Eyes: Maine Coon, brown classic tabby.

COLOURS

General Considerations—In all colours the underparts will be lighter than the back. In kittens and adolescents, allowances should be made for faint

precluding the award of challenge certificate.

Brown (Breed 27): In maturity the adult should be a rich warm seal brown, shading almost imperceptibly to a slightly lighter shade on the underparts; apart from this and slightly darker ears and mask, there should be no shading or marking of any kind. Very dark colour, bordering on black, is incorrect. Nose leather rich brown, foot pads brown.

Blue (Breed 27a): In maturity, the adult should be a soft silver grey, only very slightly darker on the back and tail. There should be a distinct silver sheen on rounded areas such as ears, face and feet. Nose leather very dark grey, foot pads pinkish grey.

Chocolate (Breed 27b); In maturity, the overall colour should be warm milk chocolate. Ears and mask may be slightly darker, but legs, tail, and lower jaw should be the same colour as the back.

Evenness of colour very desirable. Nose leather warm chocolate brown, foot pads a brick pink shading to chocolate.

Lilac (Breed 27c): In maturity, the coat colour should be a pale delicate dove-grey, with a slightly pinkish cast giving a rather faded effect. Ears and mask may be slightly darker in colour. Nose leather lavender pink, foot pads shell pink in kittens, becoming lavender pink in adults.

Red (Breed 27d): In maturity, the coat colour should be light tangerine. Slight tabby markings may be found on the face, and small indeterminate markings elsewhere (except on sides and belly) are permissible in an otherwise excellent cat. Ears should be distinctly

The standard calls for the head of the Burmese to be slightly rounded on top, with good breadth between the ears.

darker than the back. Nose leather and foot pads pink.

Brown Tortie (Breed 27e): Normal tortie. The coat should be a mixture of brown and red without any obvious barring. The color and markings are not so important as the Burmese type, which should be excellent. Nose leather and foot pads plain or blotched, brown and pink.

Cream (Breed 27f): In maturity, the coat colour should be rich cream. Slight tabby markings may be found on the face, and small indeterminate markings elsewhere (except on the sides and belly) are permissible in an otherwise excellent cat. Ears should be only slightly darker than the back coat colour. Nose

leather and foot pads pink.

Blue Tortie (Breed 27g): Blue cream. The coat should be a mixture of blue and cream without any obvious barring. Colour and markings are not so important as the Burmese type, which should be excellent. Nose leather and foot pads plain or blotched, blue and pink.

Chocolate Tortie (Breed 27h): The coat should be a mixture of chocolate and red without any obvious barring. The colour and markings are not so important as the Burmese type, which should be excellent. Nose

Facing page: The Burmese's eyes can be any shade of yellow, from chartreuse to amber, with golden yellow being the preferred color.

Scale of Points	General	All Torties
Body shape, legs, tail, feet	30	35
Body colour, coat texture & condition	25	20
Head and ears	20	20
Shape and set of ears	15	15
Colour of eyes	10	10
Total	100	100

leather and foot pads plain or blotched, chocolate and pink.

Lilac Tortie (Breed 27i): The coat should be a mixture of lilac and cream without any obvious barring. The colour and markings are not so important as the Burmese type, which should be excellent. Nose leather and foot pads plain or blotched, lilac and pink. **Note**—In the case of the four tortie colours 27e, 27g, 27h and 27i, the coat may display two shades of its basic colours and may thus appear to display three or even four colours. The colours may be mingled or blotched; blazes, solid legs or tails are all permissible: therefore, additional marks are awarded for type, which is of far greater importance than coat colour and markings.

Facing page: The ears of the Burmese are set far apart, emphasizing the breed's keen and alert expression.

COMMENT ON THE STANDARD

It will be understood by the reader that the standard in isolation of a firm mental image of the Burmese is quite worthless, as it is, of necessity, a guide only and as such is open to considerable interpretation by breeders and, of course, judges. A standard can never be absolute because no two cats could fit such a standard, and one must always bear in mind the word "balanced." The back length of one Burmese may, in real terms, be longer than that of another, but, provided its legs are proportionately longer and its head larger, then overall balance is retained. Phrases such as "slightly rounded," "set well apart on the skull" or "Ears should be medium in size" can only take on meaning to the beginner after a great number of quality Burmese have been seen; only then can one decide if trends are moving towards extremes of the standard or staying broadly within its meaning.

One of the major problems in Burmese is that in relation to its overall shape, for on the one side there are the quite full-faced and heavier American types, while on the other there is the slimmer, more foreign or oriental shape typical of British and Australian Burmese. Both are equally attractive, though it would seem to me that the American type is more at

Body studies:A Devon Rex, brown mackerel tabby, and a Japanese Bobtail, tortoiseshell and white.

risk of losing its type to appear more as a British Shorthair.

It would seem to this author that the standard in respect of the torties is less than desirable for, by implication, to award lower points for colour and more for type suggests that colour in the other varieties is more important than is body shape, which is not the case. The number of points for body shape in the self colours is still, of course, greater, but the ratio of the points is lower. It is important to remember that body type is body type, and when one starts to apply differing points based on colour, it does strike me as a classic case of applying "double standards."

CHARACTER OF THE BURMESE

The Burmese cat shares with its many cousins, variously labelled as "Foreign," several characteristics. For one thing, they are extremely intelligent, and this shows up in many facets of their personality. They are always investigating things, and if you hear a sudden crashing of pots and pans, it is usually the cat climbing in cupboards or attempting to explore places not intended for exploration! Their claws seem longer than in many non-foreign breeds, and they are quite willing to try their hand at curtain climbing. These sort of goings-on may not appeal to everyone, so if you are looking for a lap cat that does little else but sit with you, then a Burmese may prove to be a handful. These are very playful cats who remain kitten-cats throughout their lives.

They are extremely affectionate felines that will fill a dual role—little horrors one minute and then loving the next. They will wrap themselves around your neck or sprawl over your chest and happily gaze into your eyes as they purr away and "knead" into your jacket or sweater. I do not suggest that other breeds do not do these things, but Burmese certainly don't believe in doing anything by halves! If they are causing mischief, they do it with style. One belonging to my mother was adept at opening the fridge door—thus helping itself to meals whenever the urge to eat came over it. They can learn to open catches on windows, open boxes and generally gain entry to anything or place not really secured.

A feature of this breed is the range of "voices" it has, some of which really verge on the eerie. It is a breed that will fit into home life very well, for they enjoy the company of people, at times apparently more so than that of their own kind. They get on fine with dogs and with other cats, but sometimes other breeds find them a bit of a handful, as they are forever wanting to play and will find new ways of creeping up on their companions.

Selecting a Burmese

The decision to acquire a Burmese is certainly a very good one, but before purchase is actually made, the potential owner should consider a number of points that have importance, depending on why the Burmese is wanted in the first place. Basic to everything is that each member of the family

A healthy Burmese, or any other breed of cat, will have clear sparkling eyes and a clean nose and ears.

should be consulted to see if they are as enthusiastic as you are to own this breed. Assuming everyone approves, then the likely questions you will be pondering are as follows:

1. Is the cat required as a pet or do you envisage breeding and showing Burmese?
2. Is a male or female the better choice?
3. What is the best age to acquire a kitten?
4. Where is the best place to purchase this breed?
5. How can one tell if the kitten is healthy?
6. What paperwork is needed?

We will discuss each of these questions before dealing with the practical aspects of feeding and general management in the chapters that follow.

PET, SHOW OR BREEDING

There is a clear distinction between the make-up of a Burmese that is only required as a pet as compared with one that may be taken to exhibition or bred. Clearly, a show cat must be of a high standard in relation to its physical features, and such cats will obviously command greater prices than would a Burmese that is only to be a household companion. In the latter case, you still obviously want a typical specimen of the breed, but a small fault that might preclude the cat from exhibition honors will in no way detract from its charm as a family pet. Such a cat may still have quality breeding behind it, so it will have the same sort of character as will the biggest show winner around.

A cat with which one would like to start breeding operations will be of good quality, though it may not itself be superb from a show point of view. Many excellent tomcats have shown their ability to pass on good qualities, though they may not have hit the high spots on the show circuit.

Likewise, a good sound and typical queen does not need to be an all-out beauty in order to be an excellent foundation cat from which to build a strain. However, breeding cats do need to come from a genuine strain where there is a proven record of producing very consistently typical examples of the breed; again, such cats will not come cheaply. With Burmese, as with most things in life, you will get what you pay for, and bargains rarely occur.

Should you purchase a cat essentially as a pet but then later decide you would like to breed or maybe exhibit, then you are strongly advised to purchase another cat with this in mind rather than attempt to build a line using a pet-quality animal. This might well be cheaper initially, but progress will be harder and it will work out to be far more expensive in the long run, when you might still have to cut your losses and start again from scratch.

MALE OR FEMALE

In terms of the family pet, it does not matter which sex you purchase because both make loving and playful companions. It will be more in the nature of the individual, rather than its sex, as to its character. There are really boisterous queens and there are very placid toms, so it is a case of observing the kittens on offer to you and trying to select one which displays the sort of temperament you are looking for. In seeing the kitten, you are almost certainly seeing the adult, for a sluggard at this age will be much the same when it matures; likewise the little hooligan at eight weeks of age will likely be just as cheeky when it becomes an adult.

However, when studying kittens, one must be aware that even at this age they have their on and off days, so this must be taken into account when making judgments. Thus the seller is in a much better position to advise you which are the get-up-and-go types and which ones are more sedate. The idea of always opting for the most lively is not the best way to select a Burmese, if you are the sort who is looking for a quiet cat that does not want to play all of the time. Cat psychology is still very much in its infancy, but it is possible to predict, with

If you are interested in showing, you will want to select a Burmese whose physical features measure up to those noted in the standard.

reasonable accuracy, likely activity rating within litters of kittens.

If you do plan to have a pet only, then you are urged to have it spayed or neutered at the appropriate age.

AGE TO PURCHASE

As far as kittens are concerned, this is a thorny question, since experts differ greatly in what they consider to be a suitable age. I will briefly ponder the various schools of thought and then offer my own attitude to the question.

The Governing Council of the Cat Fancy (GCCF) recommends that pedigreed cats not leave their mothers until they are 13 weeks of age, and many breeders support this view. The basis behind this is that, until this age, the kittens need to socialize with their own kind and still need the companionship and teaching qualities of their mother. To remove them at an early age will induce stress, which in turn lowers their ability to cope with disease at this crucial time in their lives.

The opposing thought is that the longer the kitten stays with its mother and litter mates, the more it will relate to cats rather than to humans, so it will not integrate within another family quite as well as if it had been acquired at an early age. Further, if it is within a cat establishment, then clearly it is exposed to

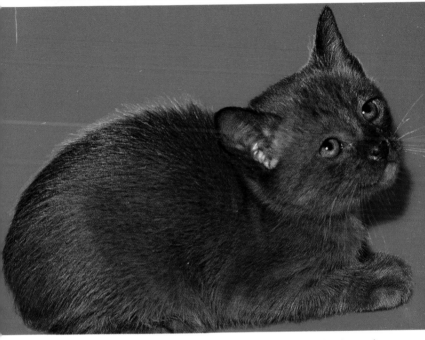

A lovely sable Burmese kitten. In general, a kitten who is shy and retiring will likely be much the same way as an adult. Observe the behavior of your prospective pet very carefully, so that you can know what to expect when he grows up.

potential illness in a ratio to the number of other cats being kept, so it does not automatically follow that it is less likely to develop an illness if retained with its mother. The permutations are many, and I think factors such as the purchaser's own previous experience with cats is of importance when deciding on age to purchase. Another factor is whether there are very young children in the home, for, if so, an older kitten would seem the wiser choice. Likewise, whether other pets are kept might influence the preferred age, so that I do not think it is possible to say that a young kitten of seven or eight weeks of age is better than one of 12-14 weeks, or vice versa, without taking other factors into account.

For ourselves, we normally try to acquire kittens when they are about eight weeks old and have never taken on a cat

A Burmese mother cat and her litter. Never purchase a kitten under eight weeks of age, as it will not have had enough time for socialization with its siblings.

beyond 12 weeks of age (other than strays that adopt us!). By eight weeks they should be weaned onto solid foods and are quite steady on their feet, so they are by now independent of their mother yet young enough to socialize well with humans. Much past 12 weeks it is pot luck how well they adjust to fresh sounds, and much depends on how well the seller has socialized them to familiar sounds and objects. In actual fact, much of the kitten's character has been determined by the age of about four or five weeks, because it is influenced by sound from the moment it is born, and once its eyes start to open after the ninth day or so, then stimuli increase rapidly. You will thus be controlled as much by the seller's attitude and the impression you give, as to your own capabilities, as to any known criteria on the matter.

WHERE TO PURCHASE

Many people think of their local pet shop as the first source for a pedigreed cat, and very often they're right. However, no pet shop can possibly stock all breeds of cat. If your pet dealer does not have a Burmese available, he will often be able to help you locate a reputable breeder. If he is unable to assist you, locating a Burmese breeder is not difficult, for you can write or telephone the national or local registration association for cats, and these will advise you of any specialty clubs or all-breed cat societies in your area. The secretaries of these clubs will then supply you with names and addresses. Cat magazines can be ordered from your local supplier, or you could ask your local veterinarian. Many pet shops will be excellent sources of information, and apart from that they will be able to supply most of your cat needs over the coming years. Finally, the very best way to contact breeders is to attend a number of cat shows, where you will not only see all the different colors available but will meet many breeders all in one location.

The amount of research you do will reflect just how involved you wish to become with the breed, for the potential breeder will need to consider very carefully the proven record of the breeder who is to supply the foundation stock. With this in mind, it is better if such a person is not too far away from your home, so that you can visit him/her more easily if you have problems or if you wish to buy additional stock from them at a later date.

THE HEALTHY BURMESE

The first that can be said with regard to a kitten's health is that if you have purchased from a reputable source, then

A male cream Burmese, one year old.

the animal's health will be good. Such a breeder simply would not allow a less-than-fit kitten to leave his care. Should you have selected a Burmese while it was still very young and arranged to collect it at a later date, then you can always ask the seller if he/she will arrange for a veterinary health certificate to be available on the day of collection; you will have to pay the extra fee involved, but you will have the safeguard of knowing that a vet had examined the kitten within 24 hours of your acquiring it.

Failing this, then you should arrange for a veterinary examination of the kitten within 24 hours of your taking it home; the former, however, is better.

A healthy kitten is not difficult to identify—nor is one that is unwell. First of all, you should watch the kitten at play; it should move about without any signs of impediment. Some kittens are more active than others, so the slower kitten is not necessarily ill, though one which shies away and hides in a corner habitually has some sort of a problem—be it healthwise or psychological—so is not a good choice. After watching the kittens a while at a distance, they can then be examined close in hand.

The eyes should be round, within the breed limits, and should be clear and sparkling, with no

Burmese babies. Every Burmese is an individual with a personality all its own.

signs of weeping or staining that might suggest a cold or other problems.

The ears should be erect, clean on their inner surfaces and showing no signs of dirt inside them. They, nor the kitten itself, should exhibit no odors other than a typical and pleasant smell that is common to all young animals.

The teeth will be very small but white, and the mouth and tongue will be pink.

The fur will be short, smooth and sweet smelling. Brush it with your hand against its lie in order to check that there are no signs of lice, fleas or ticks. These tend to congregate around the back of the ears, at the tail root or on the underparts. They are easily spotted.

The body should feel

supple with no lumps whatsoever; gently press the abdomen for such signs, and also run your hands down the front and rear legs to check that the bones feel nice and firm with no projections to them. The tail should have no kink in it towards or at its tip, as this is a fault in all foreign type breeds (or in any cat for that matter).

The pads of the feet will be supple to the touch with no signs of hardness or sores on them.

The rectal area beneath the tail should show no signs of staining, which would indicate any number of possible causes, from simple digestive problems to very serious conditions.

As far as color goes, the color of kittens will be lighter than in the adult, so that faint tabby markings may well be seen. In light-colored varieties these may well be evident into maturity. This is not, of course, a health matter.

Finally, when the kittens are at play, it is often useful to see which ones tend to come to you rather than stay at a distance—one that chooses you rather than the reverse is not always a bad thing, especially if we are talking in purely pet terms.

THE PAPERWORK

When you collect the kitten you will be supplied with its pedigree, which may indicate three to five

A trio of Burmese. Letting your pet roam freely outdoors exposes him to a number of dangers, including his being stolen. Close supervision is necessary if you are going to let him outdoors.

generations of its lineage. A pedigree, regardless of how many champions it features, is no indication that the kitten is a quality Burmese; it is merely an indication of the line of descent, and in that sense may be a useful guide to the relative degree of inbreeding within the line. The kitten itself is the final indication of quality, and thus a pedigree is only as good as the animal which bears it—no more, no less.

You will receive the kitten's registration

papers, which will need to be sent to the registration association in order to change ownership to your own name. This is important if you plan to exhibit and breed your Burmese. Depending on the kitten's age, you may also receive a vaccination certificate which will indicate when, against what, and with which manufacturer's product the kitten has been treated. It will indicate when boosters are due and it should be taken at such times to your own vet so he knows which vaccines to use. Some breeders will supply new owners with diet sheets, and these are useful because it is always wise to maintain the same diet during the kitten's initial transition period to its new home.

Finally, if the breeder has any leaflets in respect to breed clubs, show dates and venues, or other interesting information, then by all means take the opportunity to acquire them. Maybe the kitten has an old toy it is especially fond of, or a blanket that perhaps the breeder will sell or give you. Anything that will help the kitten to settle into its new home with ease will be beneficial.

To conclude this chapter, might I suggest that you consider having not one but two Burmese. I can guarantee you will get twice as much enjoyment from them, beyond which they will provide company for each other when you are out. Of course, two Burmese can be real little tearaways when they start playing around the home—but isn't that what makes them such lovable companions?

Your Burmese needs time to get acclimated to his new home and family. Owner, Herb Zwecker.

The Burmese is in handsome company in the grouping of newer breeds of cat. This is a Javanese. Owner, Andrea Fera.

Feeding

A great deal of research has been undertaken into the nutrition of cats, and much has been written on the subject, but at the end of the day the bottom line is in understanding that a cat is a carnivore, and then applying a degree of common sense to this, when the health of your pet will be assured, at least from a nutritional standpoint. The range of prepared foods is so extensive these days that you do not need to understand about the ingredients—just how to use a can opener—and the cat will live a long and happy life.

However, as with most foods, variety adds interest. While a cat may well survive on a monotonous diet, it will certainly appreciate a change of menu; cats, like ourselves, clearly enjoy the process of eating and have individual preferences as to the foods they most enjoy. Eating habits are acquired at an early age, so that, as a kitten grows up, it will tend to eat only that with which it is familiar or which is quite natural to eat. In Western countries, for example, few cats eat rice, but in Asia most cats will eat this without problem, often because there is little else on offer, so it becomes a case of eat what you can get or starve! Such cats will greedily devour any form of protein—meat, cheese, and such—because these comprise the basic ingredients of a feline diet (cheese being an example of a by-product of herbivores).

A cat that is given only cereal foods in their various forms will lack growth and good health, but it should not be supposed that a cat fed only on fresh meat will therefore be super fit; it will certainly be stronger and fitter than those fed on spartan meat, or no-meat diets, but will still be subject to nutritional deficiency because it will lack roughage and certain vitamins in its diet. We must therefore feed our cats so that we strike a balance between the basic ingredients fundamental to the particular animal species and the auxiliary foods that are nonetheless vital to healthy body metabolism. It will be appreciated that in the wild a cat will consume most of the animal which it kills, so it will gain protein from the animal's tissue and muscle; vitamins from the liver; vegetable matter of various sorts, which is in varying stages of digestive decomposition within the prey's stomach; roughage from the fur or feathers, part of which will be eaten; and minerals from each of these bodily parts as well as from any small bone consumed as well. "How are these various ingredients used by the cat?" may well be asked, and in answering such a question we can note the foodstuffs that contain them.

PROTEIN

The cat is a carnivore, which, by definition, means it is basically a flesh-eater. Flesh is composed of protein, water and minerals; and the protein is composed of many chemicals known as amino acids. When a cat digests its food, the protein is broken down into its basic form of amino acids, and these are then rebuilt into the body tissues needed by the cat. Thus, protein is essential in developing and repairing muscle, or replacing that which is worn out as a result of muscular activity— walking, running and so on. A kitten has much body building to do, so it needs a goodly supply of protein; otherwise it will grow up with poor muscle and bone.

Good lean meat is a prime source of protein, but you should ensure that fresh meat given to your cats is fit for human consumption; otherwise there is a great risk that it may be infected with worms, flukes, or bacteria. Generally, cats prefer beef to other meats, with lamb being the second choice

and pork being the least liked meat. Chicken is an

Providing your Burmese with a nutritionally well-balanced diet will help to keep him looking and feeling his best. Your pet shop dealer stocks a wide variety of cat food. Owner, Diane Quaas-Lopez.

excellent source of protein and rarely will you find a cat that refuses it. Rabbit is also well liked. These are the usual meats most conveniently available. Fish is another protein-rich source, and we find that the oily species, such as sardines and mackerel, are the favored ones. This may, however, simply be acquired taste, because we tend to eat these fish more regularly ourselves. Whichever species is plentiful in your area will be as readily accepted. While fresh meat of high quality can be given raw or cooked, it is advised that only cooked fish be fed to your pets—and it should not be given too often because fish also contains a thiaminase that destroys natural thiamine (vitamin B1), which is essential to healthy growth.

Cooking meat likewise destroys about half of this vitamin, but in commercially prepared foods such losses are compensated for by the addition of supplements after the cooking has been completed. In the case of meat cooked in your home, you can overcome cooking losses of vitamins by the addition of yeast powder or tablets given periodically to your cats, and by the addition of one-half ounce of cod liver oil to the diet once a week. This will ensure ample vitamin content, especially if your cats do not drink much milk or eat liver, both of which are rich in vitamin A, which is vital to cats as they are unable to synthesize this in their bodies.

Fats are usually in association with meats, and while it is not advisable to feed a large quantity of fats as a cheap substitute for good meat, nonetheless fat is required for good body metabolism. Within the body it aids the absorption of vitamins, especially vitamin A. Fat converts readily to energy, and excess needs are deposited in the body to provide insulation. There is evidence that the fat needs of kittens are high and far more important than that of cereals in young animals. A small piece of cooking lard, or that fat which is residual (dripping) after cooking meat, can be given to young cats; this should ensure good growth. Supply it each day during the first few weeks, but in very small amounts added to the meat.

VITAMINS AND MINERALS

The need for vitamins is generally appreciated by most people these days, but what is not always understood is that you can give an excess of these to your cats, and if you do they can be counter-productive and actually create health problems. This is certainly so in the case of vitamins A and D, and this same comment applies to supplements of minerals.

If your pet receives a balanced and varied diet, there should be no need to think in terms of vitamin and mineral additives, which should be given only under veterinary guidance. The exception to this comment is where fresh meats (cooked or raw) are given to kittens or pregnant females, for these will lack the amount of calcium and phosphorous needed to create strong healthy bones in the kittens and to produce milk in the females. Prepared foods are supplemented to ensure a good calcium/phosphorous ratio (ideally about 1:1). Fresh foods should be supplemented in the amount of about 5g per kg of meat given; if you are in doubt, consult your vet. There are numerous prepared cat and dog milk powders specially formulated for young animals, and these contain clear instructions for their use on the packets or cans. It can be mentioned that cow's milk is not actually the ideal milk to feed kittens, because its composition is not comparable to that of a carnivore, so formulated cat milks are always better—as is evaporated milk, which is diluted by 50% with water.

CARBOHYDRATES

Carbohydrates are not as important to cats as they are to other animals, and an excess given mixed in with meat will result in the loss of palatability of the meal. These compounds are an inexpensive source of energy but not such a refined fuel source as is fat. Examples are cereals and their products, such as bread, cookies and the like, as well as breakfast cereals. Canned dog foods contain a higher ratio of carbohydrate to meat than do cat foods, which is why cat foods always appear more expensive. It is thus false economy to feed your Burmese with prepared dog foods that contain large amounts of cereal.

Cereals contain protein, fats and vitamins, which

Protein, carbohydrates, vitamins, and minerals are important elements in the diet of your Burmese. Growing kittens especially need these compounds for good body growth and development.

is why feral cats found in such places as Spain, the Arab countries and other places not noted for their feline welfare are able to subsist on a diet that is often basically of these compounds found in rubbish bins. However, the amounts of protein in cereals is very low, and certain amino acids are missing from them. Plant proteins are also more difficult for cats to digest than those of animal origin. However, breakfast cereals and bread, both soaked in milk, will provide fiber, which is of benefit to the digestive system of cats.

FRUIT AND VEGETABLES

These foods are, of course, essentially composed of water—up to 98% by weight in some instances—but they are rich in vitamins and also contain protein and carbohydrates in varying quantities (always extremely small, though). They are not essential at all to a cat, though grasses are eaten quite naturally by felids in order to help cleanse their digestive systems periodically; they induce vomiting, and this should not be confused with a cat being sick.

Certain plants, such as seaweed, are the basis for numerous tonics in the form of powders in which many breeders have great faith, especially in relation to the extra bloom that is claimed for the coat. Generally, provided they are used in moderation, any natural herbs or fruits are likely to be of benefit,

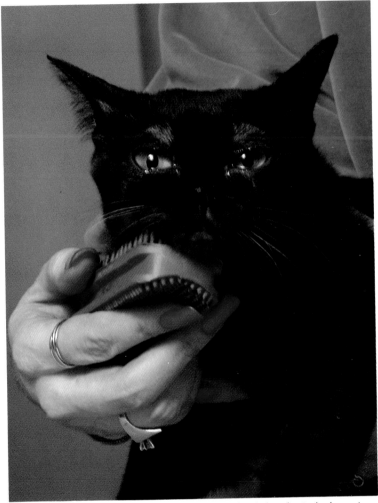

The grooming needs of the Burmese are minimal. Its short sleek coat can be kept in tiptop shape with an occasional *light* brushing. Owner, Diane Quaas-Lopez.

because they will be selectively eaten by cats in the wild either directly or via the stomach contents of the cat's prey.

WATER

A cat's body is composed of about 75% water, so it is clearly a very important requirement. It is obtained both directly when drunk and indirectly as a result of metabolic processes which release it as a by-product of the breakdown of foods, all of which contain water in differing amounts. Fresh water must always be available to your Burmese because, although it may have no need to drink much (which will be determined by how much water it receives via moist foods or milk), it should be

there when it is wanted. Some cats rarely appear to drink clean tap water yet will readily drink from puddles and other sources. This may often reflect the state of your local supply, which is treated with many chemicals, certain of which may taste quite unpleasant to a cat. As any aquarist will tell you, water that is not moving, i.e., in a bowl, very quickly goes "off" just as food can—which is why it should be replaced daily.

AMOUNTS TO FEED

It is not possible to be specific when talking about the amount of food a kitten or adult cat will require, because this will depend on a large number of factors. Quantities quoted here should take account of these, which in effect means that only by a degree of trial and error will you eventually come to know what your individual cat's needs are.

Food is used to build tissue, but its other role is to provide fuel for energy and to keep the various body systems working. The most basic of these is the pumping of blood around the body and the intake of air by breathing. These are the essentials, along with the energy needed, in order for the other internal organs to function. Everything else is an "extra," as it were, and will be very variable. For example, if you live in a cold northern climate, you will need more fuel to keep warm than if you live in the tropics. The cat's body is exactly the same, so food is needed to provide insulation and to induce shivering (though you will not see your cat doing this). The minute you move you use energy that must be derived from some source, so clearly the more often or quicker you move, the more energy is consumed— thus more fuel (food) is needed to replenish that used; otherwise you will have a negative balance and start to get thinner. Conversely, if more fuel is being taken in by the body than is being burnt up, you will have an excess which will be stored, and you grow fat.

It will be appreciated that a growing cat will be using up much more energy relative to its size than will an adult, for the kitten not only has to maintain muscle but must also be adding to this continually in order to grow. The basic systems in a kitten are more rapid than in an adult (internal pumping of the blood, kidney action and so on), so again much energy is expended and, finally, kittens are extremely active when young, so again burn up much fuel. At the peak growth period, the kitten's food intake will be greater than that required when it actually reaches maturity.

The final aspect to feeding theory is in regard to the ratios of one type of food to another. You will be aware that some fuels burn better than others; food is just the same, so that fats are the most efficient energy foods, with protein and carbohydrates about equal at 4 kilocalories per gram (kcal/g), compared to the 9kcal/g of fats. However, it happens that proteins and fats are also about the scarcest food items in the world, and are thus the most expensive. With this in mind, it is prudent housekeeping that we supply pure energy needs via the cheapest form—carbohydrates, leaving the proteins and fats to build good muscle for the body.

Care must be taken to ensure that while providing enough cheap fuels to provide energy needs, we do not skimp on the all-important proteins, especially during the growing period of a cat's life. It is better to be on the safe side and ensure a

Burmese can be just as mischievous as any other kind of feline...Everything within paw's reach is fair game. Be particularly careful with houseplants, as some can be poisonous to your pet.

sufficient quantity of protein and fats, even though this means some will be wasted in conversion to purely body fueling purposes; you get only the one opportunity to build substance into an animal and that is while it is young; it can never be fully added at a later date.

A reasonably sound basis for assessing total food requirement per day is that the kitten should receive about 20% of its own body weight, and this should be spread over four or five feeds at the age of about 16 weeks. If the kitten is, for example, 400g (15 oz), then it will need 80g of food per day, this to include meat, fats, carbohydrates and milk. Such a young kitten should be given a large proportion of meat and little of cereals, and the meat itself should be good lean meat rather than offal, heart, kidney or other organs—liver being given in very small amounts mixed in with the meat.

Feeds can be alternated between meat meals and milk meals in which cereals have been added. As the kitten grows, so the ratio of food to body weight will fall, and by the time the animal has attained one year of age, it will need only about 10% of its body weight in food per day. A cat weighing about 4.5kg (10 lb) will thus consume food at the rate of 450g per day. As a guide, the regular canned meat contains about 410g, with the smaller cans containing about half this amount. The cat will thus eat about .5-.75 of the regular sized can, with the additional weight taken up by milk, dry biscuit foods, and water.

An active cat will require (as an adult) canned foods which contain increased cereal content (because they are burning up fuel), while the lethargic cat is better fed with the all-meat brands. This lazy character is using little energy and so needs high protein foods to sustain and repair worn tissue, rather than providing fuel for activities it is not performing.

The important thing about feeding is to let your cat's condition be your guide. A Burmese should have good muscle; it should not look thin like many Siamese often do. It must be lithe, not fat, and its coat should sparkle. If a kitten has eaten its food with relish and is clearly looking for more, then by all means give it a little more—at this age they are soon satisfied and tend not to eat more than nature requires of them. The little piggy Burmese types come later, and it is then that you can apply more control over what you allow them to consume.

Cats always prefer small but regular meals rather than large meals. A guide with a kitten will be as follows:

8-12 weeks of age, 5-6 meals per day; 13-16 weeks, 4-5 meals; 17-30 weeks, 4 meals; over 30 weeks, 3-4 meals; over 52 weeks, 2-3 meals.

Pregnant females will

need four or five meals per day, and this same number will be required by the elderly cat who is not able to cope with quantity as it did in its younger days.

Of the fresh foods, meat and fish have already been mentioned, but cats are very partial to cheese of various flavors, scrambled egg, raw eggs (with the whites removed), gravy stock poured onto wholemeal bread, meat extracts, cured meats such as ham, tongue, corned beef, and similar protein-based foods. In terms of milk feeds, soaked bread, many forms of milk puddings (rice, semolina, etc.) and even custard are liked on an individual basis. A few vegetables can by all means be added, including potato and rice, but care should be taken that these do not reduce the appeal of the basic food which might thus be wasted. The more variety that is fed, the less likely there will be any particular vitamin or mineral deficiency.

Of the prepared foods, canned meat is both convenient and well recommended for its quality. Beware of dented cans offered without labels at a discount price. The dried biscuit type complete cat foods are excellent and have the advantage of being safe to leave down, as they do not attract flies nor do they sour as quickly. When feeding this type of food, *ample water must be available*. We use them not as complete meals but as in-between snacks, when they are greatly appreciated. You can purchase both moist packeted cat food and deep-frozen foods for cats, and both have their devotees; in the latter case, ensure that they are really well thawed out first. It can be very tempting to use prepared foods continually, but this is not sound policy because cats like a change and, in any case, biting into good fresh meat is good exercise for the cat's jaws. Too much soft food induces tooth tartar.

Contrary to popular opinion, milk is not an essential of a feline's diet. It can cause diarrhea in cats of any age.

General Management

Looking after one or more cats is very simple compared to the situation with many other pets, and this is because cats are very independent creatures; for a goodly part of the time they are quite happy doing their own thing, exploring the garden and immediate neighborhood, checking

Cats are very independent creatures, but they still need their owners' care and attention if they are to be healthy, happy pets. Grooming, proper diet, and regular veterinary care are vital to your Burmese's well-being.

out every nook and cranny in your home, or simply lazing about on a sunny window ledge, which they love to do. They will, of course, enjoy spending time with the family, so that in every way they are ideal pets.

It is always wiser to shop around and purchase the cat's

Even though your pet can do very well if he is alone much of the time, he will enjoy the companionship of another cat, with whom he can play. Many cat fanciers maintain that caring for a pair of cats is just as easy as caring for one cat.

necessities in advance of its arrival so that you have the time to decide whether this or that product is your preferred choice. Today, cats are extremely well catered to, and there is an extensive range of products available. We will look at those which are considered to be basic essentials.

LITTER TRAY AND SCOOP

Cats are extremely clean animals in their personal habits, and if you provide them with a litter tray it will be fastidiously used. It is probable that your Burmese will already be litter-trained by the time you bring it home, as training will have been instilled into the kitten from an early age.

Litter trays come in a range of sizes and colors, and you can also purchase those which have a dome over the tray to provide

Cats are very clean animals and appreciate a clean toilet area. Change the litter and disinfect the litter tray on a regular basis.

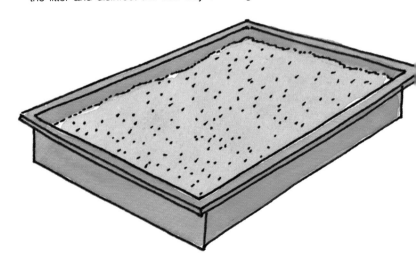

A sable Burmese female kitten, age four months.

privacy—which cats appreciate at such times!

The essential considerations of a litter tray are that it be large enough for the cat to move around in, and deep enough to retain the litter when the cat scratches at this to bury its feces. You can purchase various grades of litter, and in small or large quantities. Should you run out of litter, then sand and soil will be a suitable

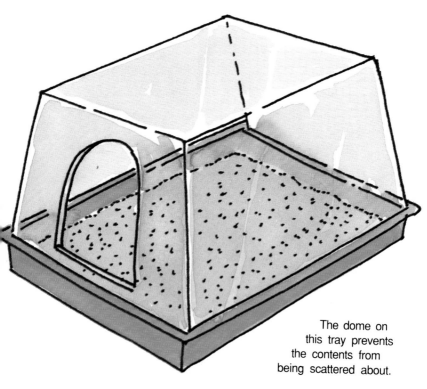

The dome on this tray prevents the contents from being scattered about.

If you do not keep your cat's litter tray clean, he may choose to relieve himself in another area of the house.

cannot keep their toilet clean. Given the free run of your yard or garden, cats will attend to their needs outside, but a litter tray is useful for overnight use or for the elderly Burmese who may be less inclined to venture out on cold or wet days.

alternative.

It is most important that once a cat's tray has been soiled, the litter is scooped up and removed; not only will this prevent an odor, but cats do not like to use soiled trays, and thus may be tempted to use alternative sites if you

When training a kitten to a tray, simply lift it up

and place the animal in it the moment you see it preparing to defecate; scolding the kitten after the event has happened is a futile exercise that it just will not understand. Do be sure to disinfect any floor areas where the kitten has deposited its wastes, because otherwise the scent might induce the animal to use the same place again. Remember, a kitten has no control over its bowel movements; this comes with maturity.

FEEDING DISHES

Feeding bowls are made of plastic, aluminum or earthenware (crock)—the latter two are

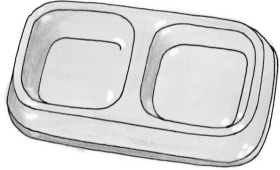

Pet shops have dog and cat dishes of every size and description.

Cats must claw like dogs must chew. If you don't have a scratching post to which your cat is trained, it will take your favorite chair (because it smells like you) and do its clawing there.

the best, though more expensive. They will last longer and do not scratch, so they can be kept spotlessly clean. Crock dishes, being heavier, do not skate across the floor as easy as do the other two. You will need separate dishes for food and water, or these can be purchased as a combined unit.

SCRATCHING POST

It has been discussed how important it is for a cat to keep its claws sharp, so a scratching post will save a lot of wear on your furniture or carpets. Of course, the outdoor cat will use trees to scratch, but cats also instinctively scratch after they have had a long nap. The post must be firm so it does not give way under the animal's efforts, otherwise your pet will not use it. It can be screwed to a wall at a convenient spot or it can be freestanding. A block of wood covered with old carpet or sacking is all that is needed. Simply place the kitten against the post and gently hold its paws in a scratching position on the post—do this a few times and kitty will get the message.

CARRYING BASKET OR CRATE

An essential item for any cat owner is a carrying basket, because there will always be

Facing page: Cat scratching posts are available from pet shops. These are mandatory, for Burmese love to climb...and a cat post is better than your drapes. Cats claw at almost anything to wear down their nails.

Carrying baskets are available at pet shops.

Pet shops have a full range of pet carriers. They are very useful for traveling and for restraining your Burmese for any reason.

occasions when it is required that your Burmese be transported somewhere: to the vet, to a show, when moving, on vacation and so forth. Beyond this use, there may also be times when you wish to restrict the cat for some reason, so a carrying basket is an important item on your initial shopping list. Baskets come in a range of shapes, sizes, and materials, which include wicker, plastic, fiberglass, wood, and aluminum. The first two named are difficult to keep clean, while the last two can get very hot, even allowing for adequate ventilation slits, so I would say that a good fiberglass model is the best choice. These are light, strong, and can be easily cleaned. Do ensure that you purchase one of suitable size so your Burmese is not cramped inside.

Getting a cat familiar with a carrying basket is no problem. Firstly, leave the basket at any spot in your home. The cat's normal curiosity for anything new will be aroused and it will soon be curled up asleep in it. We have also found it useful to have a dog crate. These are made of welded wire and can be collapsed flat; they are available in many sizes, and a big one gives your cat much more room than a carrying basket. Another useful means of transporting a cat in your car is one of the cheaper rabbit hutches. These are made of thin wood and are long, and have the benefit of accommodating a litter tray.

GROOMING AIDS

Your Burmese comes complete with a short glossy coat, so grooming is really easy when compared to the breeds with long hair. Because the coat does not tangle or pick up other than small grasses, your cat will enjoy a daily grooming, which, in spite of the short coat, is still recommended because it gives you the opportunity to keep your eyes peeled for any signs of lice or fleas. These creepy crawlies are no respecters of status, and even if you live in a palace your Burmese can still pick up fleas on its travels.

You should have a medium and fine-toothed comb, either as separate items or the sort which are double sided. A medium stiff brush will also be useful, and a good chamois leather or a piece of silk will give that final polish to the coat. A metal comb and a bristle brush, rather than plastic in each case, will cost a little more but are preferred as they do not create as much static electricity, which tends to raise the coat from its normal lie. Your Burmese should be groomed daily from the time it is taken home; be

gentle in doing this so it becomes a pleasurable experience that the cat really enjoys.

While grooming, check over the ears, eyes, teeth, and foot pads to see these are clean and show no signs of problems. The ears can be wiped clean by dipping cotton swabs into olive oil or a similar lotion; do *not*, however, probe into the inner ear, as this might set up an irritation. Dirt deep in the ear should be referred to your veterinarian to remove. Feline toothpastes are available, but you can simply rub the teeth carefully with a bit of cloth on your finger, which has been dipped into a salt and water solution. Built-up tartar can be de-scaled by your

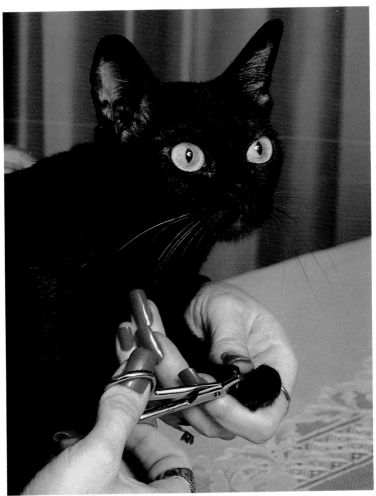

If your cat is kept indoors, it will not have a chance to wear down its claws. The claws must then be trimmed. Owner, Diane Quaas-Lopez.

Pet shops have a wide selection of cat beds in many colors and sizes.

veterinarian, though if you are feeding your Burmese correctly this should rarely, if ever, be necessary and is indicative of too much sloppy food.

Gently wipe any dirt in the corner of the cat's eyes with warm water on a cloth.

CAT BEDS

The choice of beds for your Burmese is wicker, fiberglass, bean-bags or simply a cut down

Facing page: A cat carrier can also be used as a cat bed. The cat can be penned up in this carrier whenever you don't want it to roam (like at night when you have a burglar alarm set to go off when there is perceptible movement). Owner, by Diane Quaas-Lopez.

cardboard box. Again, wicker can be a problem because fleas, lice, and mites can live unnoticed for long periods in its crevices. These creatures do not like fiberglass at all, so this is a good product. Cats like bean-bags (with washable or easy wipe covers) because they can mold them to a nice snug shape. In spite of how expensive a bed you purchase for kitty, it will still be found to favor a chair, your bed or any other sleeping spot other than that purchased for it. Indeed, an amusing aspect of all felines is that if, after you have emptied

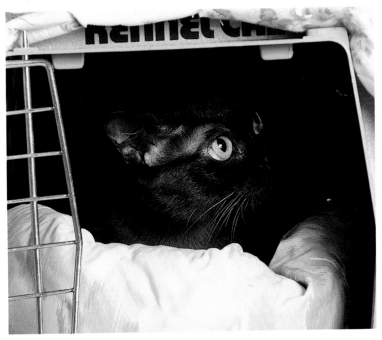

This is like a dog's bed except much smaller. Cats accept this style too.

your groceries from the cardboard box they were in, you leave this box on the kitchen floor or table, it will not be long before one of your cats is sitting in it or is asleep in it. They are fascinated by anything new and will even sit on a piece of cloth placed on your living room floor. Apart from our Burmese, we have an enormous ginger tom (among others), and he looks quite ridiculous at times when he attempts to sit in a box hardly big enough for a kitten, let alone a giant feline. A cat can be encouraged to use its bed if this contains a nice wooly blanket which it can knead on, this being a habit retained by cats from their infancy when it prompted their mother to release milk. You will find your Burmese does this whenever it is getting tired and is about to settle down for a nap.

This cat bed is cave-like and "fur" lined with a soft, fluffy fabric. Cats love it.

CAT DOORS

Cat doors are small openings that have a flap contained within a frame. This is fitted near the bottom of a door, the appropriate piece of wood having been removed from the door. They can be operated as two-way or one-way entrances and are normally fitted with a magnet so that every puff of wind does not send a draft through your house. By placing the kitten through the flap a few times, it will soon know how to open it. Do bear in mind that if the cat can re-enter your home from the yard via the cat door, it just might bring home the occasional mouse or rat without your knowing, so that one way out is often the preferred arrangement. We use a different system; the cats tap the window or door and one of the family promptly leaps up to let the cat in—we have them very well organized! The

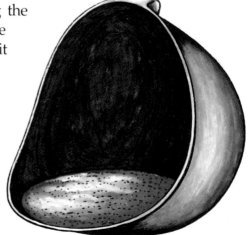

A popular kind of cat bed.

process is repeated when they want to go out, which illustrates how well cats can be trained.

COLLAR AND LEASH

Burmese are one of the few breeds of cat that actually seem to accept leash training. Of course, any cat can be trained to a leash, but they are never happy about being on one. Indeed, even Burmese would prefer to walk in freedom, for cats do not like to be restrained when in the open; they feel very vulnerable in such situations. All cats should have a collar, and this should carry a name tag, complete with your address. In many countries this is now obligatory. A cat collar is better for being elasticized so there is not the risk of the cat getting caught up on a tree branch. You can purchase reflective collars that will show up against auto headlights—this just might save a cat's life.

To train your cat to a leash, it should first be allowed to trail this behind it while in the home. The next stage is to walk it in your yard until it is quite used to the restraint of a leash. Never pull a cat along, but let it walk at its own pace. Only when it is really confident on a leash should you attempt to venture off your property. An alternative to a collar (for exercise walks only) is a harness, as this gives you more control over the cat in the event it is confronted by a dog or is otherwise startled.

I should state that, unless you live in a high-rise block, I can see no benefits in ever taking a cat for a walk. A cat is not a dog and is not at all happy being taken out of its own little territory. Even within this it is happier if going where it wants to go—and this will be via the most secured pathway; that is, a cat by inclination will avoid open spans. Should you live in the country, you will find a cat will follow you for walks but it will turn back when it reaches its territory boundary, or will continue to follow but not without "complaining" along the way, and should you get too far ahead you will need to make periodic stops until your Burmese has caught up. Cats vary in their willingness to go too far from home, and we have had a trail of cats behind us—each having its own limits. As we return down the lane, one by one each cat emerges from the hedgerows. Only the most confident go the full distance!

The foregoing covers the obvious items that your pets will need, but you will find various toys, chews, mats, and other products on display in your pet store. In addition, a ping-pong ball on string—maybe attached to the scratching post—will keep a cat amused for quite some time. Old cotton spools will be hunted and knocked around the floor, as will any similar small object. Cats love to both explore and play a sort of hide-and-seek with you, either around the furniture or in and out of a cardboard box. With a cat, all games have a hunting theme—you or the object being the hunted.

HANDLING CATS

The predisposition to be handled is both inherited and controlled by the number of times a kitten is lifted up and the manner in which this is done. Thus, it cannot be assumed that all Burmese enjoy being picked up to the same degree. A kitten roughly handled by a child may come to dislike being picked up later in life, so it is important that children are taught the correct way to handle a kitten from the moment it is first taken to your home.

The essential point is that the cat must be supported under its chest and gently lifted so that it will not fall from your hands. Never lift a kitten by the ruff of its neck, nor by just its front legs. Some Burmese are quite happy to be cradled upside down in your arms in the manner of a baby, but most do not like this form of handling and are happier just resting their front paws over your shoulder—or actually wrapping themselves around your neck. Of course, many enjoy sitting on your lap. In the case of a show cat, it is important that it is used to being held at arm's length, in the manner that will often be used by a judge. It is also important that it is quite happy having total strangers lift it up, so have friends and relatives do this when they are visiting you. A nervous Burmese will not show itself to best effect, so a show cat must be quite familiar with the hustle and bustle of people around it. This is why potential show cats should be entered into local events first, so they gain experience before progressing to larger exhibitions.

SECURITY AND SAFETY

When you arrive home with your kitten, the first thing it will want is either a small meal, a drink of water or maybe a nap. However, after this, it will soon be exploring its new home, so care must be taken that it cannot wander off or be at risk to injury. For example, a tea or coffee cup containing hot liquid could easily spill onto a kitten if kitty were to hang onto a cloth on which the cup was standing. Loose electrical wires might be bitten, or a draft from a window could suddenly cause a door to slam, trapping the kitten or its tail.

Open fires should be fitted with guards, and fish tanks equipped with canopies. Should you live in a high-rise building, then obviously the kitten should not be allowed to play on a balcony fitted with open railings. On its first day, it is better that the kitten be restricted to just one or two rooms; it can explore the rest of the home over the following days. Always be very watchful of a kitten in a kitchen, because this room holds so many dangers to such a young animal. When handling hot pots, it is better if the kitten is removed from the kitchen, where it might get under your feet and injure both of you were you to stumble over it.

Other pets must be introduced to a kitten with caution, and it is always wise to lavish extra attention on the resident pet, so that it does not come to regard the kitten as an interloper who is getting the

Your pet shop will have special harnesses and collars for cats. These are usually made of soft nylon so they won't irritate the cat.

attention formerly bestowed upon itself.

When you are out of the home, always check that doors and windows are closed; otherwise you may return to find one missing Burmese. Sadly, honesty not being what it was of old, a Burmese kitten is a very desirable animal to many people, and in some places, a lucrative trade goes on in stealing young pedigreed cats and dogs.

VACCINATION

Feline leukemia virus is one of the most frightening diseases for cats and cat lovers alike. Most victims of FeLV contract this disease when they are two to three years of age. Symptoms vary, but they often include apathy, loss of weight and appetite, fever and anemia.

As FeLV is contagious (it can even pass from a queen to her unborn kittens), cats that test positive for the virus should be isolated. Treatment versus euthanasia for the afflicted pet should be discussed with the veterinarian. When choosing a cat or kitten, it is wise to purchase from a pet shop or cattery which advertises its stock as FeLV-negative.

Recently, a feline leukemia vaccine became available. FeLV-negative cats are given an initial set of three vaccinations which are then followed by yearly boosters. These shots will save countless feline lives and prevent the heartache which accompanies the loss of a beloved pet.

Two major diseases to which cats are prone, if not fully protected by vaccination, are cat flu and feline enteritis (or panleucopenia). The former is caused by various viruses, but two are especially dangerous. Feline viral rhinotracheitis (FVRV) and feline calici (FCV) can be effectively countered by vaccinations which are given when the kitten is about nine weeks old. At this same time, a combined injection will deal with feline infectious enteritis. A repeat injection is then given three or four weeks later, and boosters are given annually. Until it has received its vaccinations (and until at least seven days after these), the kitten should be kept away from other cats and indeed from other pets which might have been in contact with infected cats. You will be supplied with the appropriate certificates by your vet, and these will be needed at certain times.

Certificates will be needed should you exhibit your Burmese, because, obviously, other owners do not want their cats exposed to unvaccinated stock any more than you do. Well-run boarding establishments will insist on sight of certificates, and these will also be needed should you move to another country.

Likewise, a breeder to whom you may take your queen for mating will also need to be sure the female has been fully protected.

In Great Britain, Australia, New Zealand and Hawaii, there are extremely strict regulations in force with respect to rabies, a dreaded disease which these particular areas are free from. Cats entering these regions are required to undergo quarantine periods because antirabies injections are not used within them. Should you reside in one of these islands, when you leave, if you are taking your cats with you, it is strongly advised that you vaccinate your Burmese against rabies, even if this is not an obligatory requirement in the country in question. Appropriate information can be obtained from your veterinarian or from the Ministry of Agriculture and Fisheries (GB) or the Wildlife Dept. (USA).

It is normally not advised, in the case of the two major feline diseases, that kittens be injected before the age of nine weeks. This is because protection is still then afforded by antibodies provided by the mother. From time to time, other diseases break out which may affect cats. These are usually well reported in the popular press, and, in any case, your vet will advise on any other vaccinations that might be recommended in your particular area. Happily,

If you have a male and a female Burmese and do not want them to breed, you should ensure that they are prevented from being able to reproduce.

these are rarely needed.

SPAYING AND NEUTERING

Unless you plan to breed your Burmese, it is advised that they be prevented from being able to reproduce. This will prevent unwanted litters of what will be crossbred kittens, as it is unlikely your pedigreed cat will by chance meet up with another Burmese. Un-neutered toms are far more prone to fight other cats in the territory; they will mark their territory, including your home, with a foul smelling (to humans anyway) liquid which they spray within their urine. An unspayed female will likely be pregnant repeatedly, and this is neither beneficial to her health nor desirable to you in having litter after litter of kittens to dispose of.

A tom can be neutered from about the age of nine months, while a queen can be spayed after she is about four months of age, though generally six months is more preferred. In both cases, the operation is straight forward and there are no after-effects to worry about. Your vet will advise you on this matter. As with vaccinations, your pet must be in good health at the time of the operation, and pregnant queens cannot be spayed if they are past their fourth week unless there are very good clinical reasons for this, which only the vet can determine.

VACATIONS

When it is vacation time, it is always better if you can arrange for a friend, neighbor or relative to drop by each day and feed your pets. The second alternative, if it is practical, is to take your Burmese with you; it will not mind this at all if it has become used to this from an early age, though clearly some cats are more nervous away from home than others. People who go camping with trailers are at an advantage because, no doubt, the cat will already treat the mobile as a home. The least desirable option is to board your cat, for not only will it wonder what is happening to it, but it will be confined and obviously open to illness risk due to the number of other cats and dogs that may also be boarding at that time.

It thus behooves you to really check out the status of a cattery, and it will be wise to be prepared to pay out top dollar if it ensures the highest standards of accommodation and hygiene. The seller of your Burmese may be willing to board your pets while you are away, and you will be happy that this will only be on a small scale, probably, offering the service only to cats they have bred or sold.

MOVING

Most people move once

or twice during the course of their lives, and at such times care must be taken to transport the family cat as comfortably as possible. Take it with you rather than having it shipped with the furniture or by a carrier. On arrival at the new house, keep the doors closed so the cat can explore. Feed it as soon as possible, as this will establish a basic relationship between the cat and the new "habitat." It must be stated that some cats just do not like to move to new homes and may decide to return to the original one. Journeys of hundreds of miles are proven facts for cats, which navigate by the sun's position and maybe by other means we do not yet fully understand. It is usual to keep the cat in the new home for 24 hours so that by then it realizes you are staying; no doubt it is comforted by familiar smells such as those that will be on the furniture and other household goods taken with you. After this period, it can be allowed into the garden to explore and, depending on whether it likes your choice, it will decide whether to stay or go. If a cat enjoys a comfortable loving home, then in almost all cases it will happily settle down.

We have had a case either way. On one occasion we moved only a few miles and one of our cats simply refused to accept the new home and

Burmese are intelligent cats. If they are allowed outside freely, they develop a love of their range and should you move to a nearby neighborhood, the cat might wander back to her old haunts. Owner, Diane Quaas-Lopez.

returned to the former one which was much more wooded and larger. In the end we allowed her to stay, as the new owners were cat-lovers; all worked out to the cat's satisfaction. We also inherited a cat in the same manner; it quite literally came with the property and had done so with the previous owners!

Breeding

If you intend from the outset to become a breeder of Burmese, then you will need to purchase one or maybe two females of very sound type. Hopefully, if your judgment has been good—and that is what breeding is all about— these will be the basis of your own strain. With this in mind, there may be merit in purchasing young adults rather than kittens. It is true you will miss out on the fun of a kitten, but then again you will have many youngsters to look forward to in the coming years. The advantage of a young adult is that its development is less uncertain than in the case of a kitten, which may not mature to the potential it appeared to have at six to ten weeks old. Of course, a good adult is going to cost much more money, but since so much will depend on the foundation stock, this is a sound investment. Such an adult may even have a few wins behind it at shows.

In the selection of breeding stock, you must not place all the attention on physical appearance, though it will form the basis of most of your judgment. Consideration must be given to the way the female has herself been bred, and ideally you want a queen that exhibits careful linebreeding so that there is a higher likelihood that she will breed true to type.

BREEDING AGE

A female Burmese may attain sexual maturity at any time after about five or six months of age, but the queen will not be physically mature until she is about nine months of age. Therefore, breeding from a young female is not to be recommended, as this will not only result in kittens which lack vigor, but may permanently damage the

Burmese lactate for about six weeks, but the kittens should be weaned by then. As soon as lactation stops, the reproduction cycle begins again. Should you so desire, and I advise against it, you can breed your cats more frequently by removing the kittens when they are about four weeks old.

full maturation process of the mother. It is also most important that only fully fit females be bred from, as pregnancy and kitten rearing make strong demands on a queen's body. If a female becomes ill at just the period she was due to be mated, then, regardless of how inconvenient this might be, the mating should be cancelled. The fact that the litter would not be born for some weeks— and thus the queen by then should be better— overlooks important aspects. From the moment an egg is fertilized, it is a developing embryo and will be affected by any medicaments given to the queen. It will not receive quite the same degree of nourishment as from a healthy mother, because the sick queen will be splitting her energy resources between feeding the embryo and fighting off the illness.

These same comments are no less true of the tomcat, which must be fully fit at the time it is used for stud. The male will mature somewhat later than a female, about nine to 12 months of age, but you will want to use an experienced Burmese on your maiden queen. This is important for other than practical reasons, because you will want to know that the stud is prepotent for his qualities. Because he looks like a fine Burmese by no means implies he will pass on his sterling quality to his offspring. He must therefore be old enough to have sired offspring, which you may know of and which bear testimony to his breeding worth. However, even this latter capability does not mean you should automatically seek the services of a prepotent tom which has also beaten every other cat out of sight in the exhibition world. The prudent breeder will seek the services of a tom that is the best available but which also has breeding lines that complement those of the queen; this may mean overlooking certain of the current big winners in favor of ensuring compatibility of genes.

ESTRUS CYCLE

The full estrus cycle in a cat is the period that commences with the female's willingness to be mated and terminates after she has weaned her youngsters and is willing to be mated again. This period normally spans about five months, and may be divided into three sections.

Estrus: The cat has two or three breeding periods during a year, these usually being January to May and July to August. During these periods the cat will be "in heat" for periods of two to six days' duration, and these periods of heat will repeat at 14-day intervals. From October through December a female will normally have no estrus periods, but if kept in heated and artificially lighted accommodation (as is usual in a home), then she will be induced to continue having estrus and may be mated during winter months.

Gestation: This is the period that follows the fertilization of the female egg and it lasts about 65 days, though this can fluctuate between extremes of 58-72. Kittens born prior to 58 days will be very premature and survival is unlikely.

Lactation: The queen will release milk for her offspring during this period and it will last for about six to eight weeks. The ending of the lactation period triggers the queen's next breeding period, unless winter is approaching when, in the wild, a female will not remate until the early spring of the following year.

Unlike a bitch who releases eggs continually while she is "in season," a cat is an induced ovulator, which means eggs are released by the queen only as a result of an outside stimulus—the male's penis. The number of eggs which will be fertilized is invariably greater than the number that reach full term as, for one reason or another, embryos are resorbed or fail to develop. The average litter of Burmese will be four to six, though the potential of live born is within the range of one to ten.

Facing page: Well-bred Burmese kittens should all look alike. If the kittens are different, then one or both of the parents is heterozygous and may produce undesirable offspring. Owner, Diane Quaas-Lopez.

MATING PROCEDURE

As the female approaches estrus, she will generally be more affectionate towards you (very noticeable in queens that may otherwise be less than attentive), and she will often roll over and make some sort of crying sounds. She will twitch her tail to one side when being stroked on her back and will also utter very unusual noises, which can be somewhat startling to a first time queen owner. She is said to be "calling" at this time, and care must be taken to keep her indoors and supervised; otherwise she will happily mate with any potential Romeo in the area.

You will have arranged for a stud beforehand and given the owner an indication of when you think its services will be required. The queen is always taken to the tom and is left with him for two to four days, during which time mating will be effected on numerous occasions. After initially rebutting his advances, the queen will eventually lie in front of him and he will mount her and bite into her neck, this all being part of the normal ritual the female expects. Copulation is quite quick in felines but is repeated many times before the female (though more often the male) decides enough is enough.

The female is then returned home but should still be watched with care, as more often than not she will still allow any other male to mate with her at this time. However, much depends on the timing of the mating, and if this has gone according to the book, then the queen will allow no other males to mate her once she is satisfied the mating was effective.

If the mating was not successful, then the queen will come back into estrus within a couple of weeks and, this being so, it is a good idea to check with the breeders beforehand whether they allow repeat matings at no extra cost. Such a service is often a courtesy but is not obligatory, thus the need to discuss it before the event. It is usually better to pay a one-time stud fee than to become involved in pick of the litter situations which can get rather complex.

PREGNANCY

The first signs of your Burmese being pregnant will be a reddish coloration to her nipples. This is known as pinking and happens at about the 20-day mark. Shortly after this, a veterinarian may be able to confirm pregnancy by careful palpation of the queen's abdomen. She will start to put on weight after about three or four weeks, at which time her appetite will start to increase. She will need extra food, spread over more meals per day. Shortly prior to birth, she may well be eating twice her normal rations, as the kittens are being fed within her body and she needs to keep up her own strength as well.

From about the fifth week into the pregnancy,

the kittens may be visible as distensions of the abdomen, but this is not always so; if only one or two kittens are being carried, they are often not apparent until almost the time of their birth. The queen's nipples will swell about seven days prior to the kittens' birth.

It can be mentioned that in the case of cats, it is possible for a litter to contain kittens which have differing fathers; this happens when two males mate a female during the same estrus. If the sires are the same color, you may never be aware this has happened—only in that the litter may show variation in quality, but even this is possible from the same father. It is more evident when colors turn up that, in theory, were not possible based on parentage. However, this sort of happening is very rare in well-run catteries.

During her pregnancy, your Burmese can be allowed normal exercise; indeed, this is beneficial, because she needs to keep her muscles in good shape in readiness for the time of birth. She will need ample milk, or a calcium powder, to ensure good bone in the kittens and for her milk production. Liver may be added two or three times per week to the diet, and this will ensure adequate supplies of vitamin A and other essential vitamins that she

Facing page: When your cat is pregnant you can feel the fullness in her body. At this time she should be handled as little as possible as you don't want her to jump from your grasp and hurt herself.

is unable to produce herself.

About ten days prior to the big event, you will notice your cat looking around for suitable places in which to have her litter, and you may be able to persuade her to a given location if you supply a suitably sized cardboard box, in which is placed a blanket covered with old towelling. The front should be cut down to allow for easy access, yet have a retaining lip high enough to restrict the kittens as they start to crawl about. The box should be placed in a darkened spot such as a cupboard. If the queen finds this snug and warm and feels secure in it, she may oblige you by using it, but not always, as cats choose the most unlikely places at times, which can range from the wardrobe to an old box in a corner, which you have planned to throw out for the last two years!

THE BIRTH

The birth of a litter may be divided into three basic stages. Firstly, the female will start to become restless and will scratch around in her box as though trying to rearrange things. She may cry out now and then and show signs of some discomfort. This stage may continue from only a few hours to as many as 24. The second stage is much shorter, lasting rarely longer than one hour—30 minutes being reasonable. This is the period when the queen is seen to be straining in an effort to assist the kitten along the oviduct. Initially, in the later stages of the first period, contractions were involuntary, but now the female has control over such contractions. This will result in the emergence of the kitten.

It may be presented head or feet first, and this is of no special account, only insomuch that if the first born is feet first, then the birth time is usually somewhat longer than for subsequent kittens.

The time interval between births can vary quite a bit and usually reflects the size of the litter. Sometimes a number will come in rapid succession, followed by a lengthy gap, which may be up to 24 hours. In other cases the interbirth period may be even across the whole litter. The third stage of birth is that relating to the expulsion of the placenta or afterbirth. This may follow shortly after each kitten, or it may be retained until just before the birth of the next. Less common is when placentas are retained and appear, for example, three in succession. The placenta is a dark, greenish black mass of jelly-like tissue. The kitten is attached to the placenta by the umbilical cord, which the mother will normally bite through after she has cleared the kitten's face of the membrane that may cover it. This membrane contained the amniotic fluid which cushioned the embryo while it was growing and ensured it of a warm environment. At birth, this fluid is expelled, the process being termed the breaking of the water bag.

It sometimes happens that maiden queens panic a little in their first litters and do not take the required action; in such cases you should not panic, but simply render assistance calmly and promptly. First, clear the kitten's face of any membrane that may prevent it from breathing, and then give it a rubbing with a towel, which should stimulate it to breathe and cry out. If you suspect a fluid blockage, hold the kitten head down and gently strip it between forefinger and thumb, in the manner of milking a cow. This

should release the fluid, which is wiped away

When the kittens reach three weeks of age, they may start to wander. Your pet shop might have a restraining pen in which you can keep the kittens until they are old enough to properly care for themselves. Owner, Diane Quaas-Lopez.

from the nostrils; the process is repeated to ensure that the respiratory tract is clear. Next, tie a knot of cotton around the umbilical cord about 1.25-1.9 cm (.5-.75 in) from the navel and, with sterile scissors, cut the cord on the placental side of the knot. In order to minimize bloodflow from the placenta, a similar knot can be tied at the same distance from the afterbirth. The kitten can now be returned to the mother or placed on a blanket near her which is covering a hot water bottle. It is useful to weigh the kittens at birth, and thence daily thereafter, as this will indicate that they are steadily gaining weight; if not, it indicates a problem.

After the first kitten is born, the queen will usually cope well enough by herself, and we are fortunate in cats since, unlike dogs, few problems are associated with births.

Should your Burmese go longer than an hour without giving birth to another kitten, yet is clearly straining to do so, you should contact your vet, as there is obviously a difficulty. Do try to check on the afterbirths so that each one is accounted for in relation to the number of kittens born. The mother will normally eat the afterbirths, but you can remove one or two before she does so. Her action in this is instinctive, for were these to lay around in the wild, they would attract potential predators and would decompose and be a health risk. Further, the mother would derive nutrition from them, for she may not have found catching prey easy in the last day or two prior to giving birth.

Of course, the queen may give birth while you are away from home, or overnight, in which case you will not be aware of what exactly happened, but in any event it is wise to have your veterinarian examine the queen just to be sure she is fine and has retained no kittens or afterbirths. Once all the litter is born, the mother will be clearly relaxed and will proudly wash each of her babies with much enthusiasm.

BIRTH PROBLEMS

Happily, the Burmese does not encounter problems as a general rule, so there is no need to discuss all the things that could go wrong. In any such instances, the first signs that something is obviously amiss should be referred to your vet; for example, loss of blood from the vagina, or obvious pain beyond the discomfort all females endure during parturition (birth). Sometimes a very large kitten may be unable to move down the oviduct, and a Caesarean may be required because the queen has either a small pelvis or one that is not quite normal. In such cases it is better to take the vet's advice as to the future breeding suitability of the female. If your Burmese has ever been involved in an accident which may have affected her rear limbs, then breeding from her is not recommended, as the pelvis may be damaged, making breeding a risky affair.

A queen may not have been mated fully yet go through all the stages of apparent pregnancy—this being termed phantom pregnancy—and the queen's nipples will pink up and she may even produce milk. The procedure is that you should advise your vet, who will confirm the absence of pregnancy and may treat the queen with antibiotics. Normally, she will in any case grow out of the phase and come back into estrus in due course, her milk drying up in a natural manner.

KITTEN REARING

During the first three to four weeks of their lives, the kittens will gain all the nourishment they need from their mother, so her diet should continue to be of the highest quality, including plenty of milk. The queen may show little interest in food for the first 24 hours after birth, but then her appetite will return. The initial milk she secretes to the kittens is called colostrum and is rich in antibodies to protect the babies from illness.

When they are born, the kittens are quite helpless and can neither see nor hear, nor can they move about other than by crawling. The eyes will begin to open at about five days of age and will be fully open at about 20 days. Their color will be a blue-gray, but this will slowly change over the following three months or so to be that of the adult Burmese. By three weeks of age the kittens will be about five or six weeks, and they start to shed them around the 16-week mark. There are only 26 milk teeth in the cat, the four missing being the molars which, as they

During the first three to four weeks of their lives, kittens get all the nourishment they need from their mother.

walking about, somewhat shakily, and within a week of this they will be able to run about.

When born, the kittens have what are termed deciduous or milk teeth, but these do not erupt for a few weeks. They are complete, however, by

erupt, are permanent.

As they reach three weeks of age, the kittens will begin to show interest in their mother's milk and food and may be encouraged to lap from a saucer, but remember that individual kittens may be more, or less, advanced than their litter mates. At four weeks, you can start to offer them tiny scrapings of meat; it can be mixed in with a milk and cereal food, and soon this will be eagerly devoured, to the point that the kittens hiss and growl at anything that comes near them. They are rather untidy eaters initially, and will need wiping after each feed.

You may start to litter-train them at any time after three weeks of age, and this is simply done. Until they have had their course of injections, they should not be allowed to wander out of your home. It is also wiser not to let them be handled by visitors who may well be interested buyers some weeks before the kittens are ready to leave your care. This is always a delicate matter, because you can hardly suggest to such people they are a health risk without offending, but the fact is they may well have been looking at other kittens that very day. An automatic rule you should always apply to yourself is washing your hands after handling other pets.

By eight weeks of age, the kittens should be about weaned from their mother and will be eating solid food meals alternated with milk feeds. They should be fully litter-trained by this time, and they should have been familiarized with everyday household sounds, such as vacuum cleaners, hair dryers and washing machines. You should be watching them carefully when they are at play so you can determine which are the lively and which are the more quiet ones. Do not forget to send off their registration papers to your ruling association.

HAND-REARING

There are occasions when it may be required to hand-feed a kitten; maybe the mother becomes very ill or, worse, she may have died. In such cases you will need a special kitten feeding bottle, though those from doll's sets will do, as will a regular medicinal dropper with a rubber end to it. During its first week of life a kitten will require milk feeds every two hours, round the clock, so hand-feeding is a time-consuming operation. In the second week the regularity of feeds can be reduced to every four hours, and thence to every six hours in the third week. The kitten-milk product must be given warm. It should be tested on the back of your hand. Do not attempt to pump milk quickly into kittens, as it may enter the respiratory tract.

FOSTERING

The alternative to hand-rearing is to foster kittens onto another cat, which may have spare teats available because this female has only a small litter herself. The younger the kittens can be fostered, the better, and it helps if they are wiped with something like butter or lard (not too much!), which will encourage the foster mother to lick them and, in so doing, accept them as her own. You do, of course, require the foster mother to have kittens of about the same age as those to be fostered.

RECORD KEEPING

Any breeder should keep detailed records of all breedings. This should indicate the sire used, number of young born, their birth weight, any problems experienced during birth, and how caring a mother the queen was. Obviously the color of the kittens should be included, as should any happenings that were unusual. The more detailed the records, the more useful they will be to you at a later date—

maybe even a few generations later—when they may help in determining the course of

A pair of Burmese...one with an angular face and the other with a round face.

a subsequent problem, or tracing a genetic fault or the occurrence of such in successive generations.

SELLING THE KITTENS

You should be thinking in terms of the kittens' sale from the moment they are born. If you are an exhibitor, you may already have one or two interested buyers; an advertisement in your local paper will also bring people to your home. Judging potential owners is never easy because sometimes the most unlikely looking characters may well make by far the best owners. Nor is financial status any guarantee that people will look after their pets as they should; indeed, when clearly not short of cash, there are always those who buy on impulse or because the idea (rather than the actual reality) of having a Burmese appeals to them at that moment. The cat is then ignored months later, whereas another couple or family with precious little cash may provide a very loving home to the kitten.

At best, selling is a matter of luck as to whether the home will indeed prove to be a good one, so it is always with much pleasure that you keep in contact with someone who purchased your kitten and is totally happy and devoted to it. When selling a kitten, it is always useful if you provide a printed or typed information sheet that gives basic instructions about feeding, so that the new owners can maintain your regimen, at least during the first few weeks.

Basic Genetics

It is not necessary to understand genetics in order to become a highly successful breeder, any more than you need to know all about mechanics in order to drive a car. However, some knowledge will be found most helpful, as it will explain a number of happenings, especially in respect to how color is determined.

The external appearance of a Burmese is determined by two basic factors, the first of which is the genetic make up of the individual; this is inherited from its parents. The second factor is how that individual is reared. The first gives the Burmese potential, the second determines how near to maximum potential is attained. It is thus possible to have a multitude of permutations between these basic factors. A poorly reared high-quality Burmese will, in fact, have the appearance of a poor-quality cat; a mediocre individual, in the right hands, can appear to be a not unreasonable looking example. However, it is in

There are two factors which determine the external appearance of a Burmese: its genetic makeup inherited from its parents and its upbringing.

their breeding behavior that their true quality will be revealed. The former cat, in spite of its poor looks, will still pass on its inherent quality; the latter cannot because it is superficial and was simply a case of the owner getting almost 100% of the cat's potential to materialize simply by excellent care of the animal.

If a breeder has an understanding of genetics and a sound attitude toward husbandry, then there is one more ingredient that is needed—indeed, is the very hallmark of a good breeder. The ingredient that separates the champion breeders from the "also-rans" is the ability to make selection from stock, for genetics without selection has little merit in practical application.

GENES—THE UNITS OF INHERITANCE

When a male sperm unites with a female egg, the fertilized unit is termed a zygote. This zygote divides to form two daughter cells, and these cells likewise divide, so that in this way growth is accomplished. However, something else happens; otherwise we would grow up to be a sort of jelly-like mass! Within each of the cells are tiny units of coded information, and each of these units tells the cell nucleus, and thus the cell, how it is to develop. The units are known as genes, and a cat has many thousands of these which, collectively, control every aspect of the animal from its external shape to such matters as thought patterns, aggression, ability to resist disease and so on. The internal workings of a cat's metabolism are also controlled by gene action.

These genes are not scattered at random within each body cell but are arranged in an orderly fashion along a central axis, which is known as a chromosome. The number of chromosomes in each species of animal is constant for that species (abnormalities excepted), so that in the dog there are 78, in the otter 38, in the hyena 40, and so on. The cat has 38, and this number is known as the diploid number, which means there are 19 chromosomes but that they are found with duplicates to themselves, so they are paired in each body or somatic cell. In the germ cells, only one of a chromosome pair is found, and this reduced number is known as the haploid number. When the germ cells unite to form a fertilized egg, the diploid number of 38 is thus restored; were this not so, the number of genes would of course double up at each new generation. Germ cells are therefore subject to a different type of cell division than are normal body cells. This need not be discussed but is mentioned in order to explain how chromosome numbers stay constant from one generation to the next.

The important thing to remember about chromosomes is that they are always in pairs, so that for every gene along the axis there is an equivalent gene on the opposing chromosome. The position of a particular gene on its chromosome is known as its locus. If, for example, gene 468 was a gene controlling color, then at position 468 on the opposing chromosome of the pair, that gene also would be controlling color. It is not known how many genes there are in the different animal species, so the numbers used here are merely to help clarify this business of a gene and its alternative gene, which is known as its allelomorph, or allele for short.

GENE ACTION

The next thing it is useful to understand is that some features are controlled by relatively few genes, which we may call major genes, while others are controlled by the combined actions of many genes. In the case of a major gene, we can quickly see its effect—as in color for example—so color can thus be changed relatively easily and the results as easily seen, thus monitored. However, when a feature is controlled by many genes, then matters are more difficult, because such

Facing page: This Balinese chocolate point is another Asian cat breed that has been overshadowed in popularity by the Burmese. Owner, Marjorie Bergen.

genes have only a modifying influence as individuals, it being their collective influence that determines the feature. This sort of gene action provides variation and is the reason why every possible permutation, from a Burmese that is wrong for about every feature to one which is superb, can thus be found. However, it is possible for both types of genes to be at work on a single feature. This is simply shown with a brown or sable Burmese, where the depth of color can vary between very dark to relatively light, though still being brown. The major gene involved is that which changes or dilutes the black color to brown, but the variation within the brown is the result of modifiers which are accumulative in their action.

The final basic thing needed to be appreciated is that the major genes have varying powers of expressing themselves. Some may totally mask the presence of others, or they may appear to blend with them to create an apparent midway situation (though this does not actually happen, as genes do not blend but always retain their own identity).

MUTATION

In the wild state, the cat has a basic tabby coloration, and this is known genetically as the normal or wild-type gene. Its existence can be seen in Burmese in the lighter-colored varieties where faint tracings are sometimes seen on the face and legs. However, every so often, and for reasons still not fully understood, a gene may quite suddenly change in the way it expresses itself; instead of displaying the normal coat color, the animal carrying the gene, or more likely one of its progeny, appears a different color. The mutation affects the chemistry of the cells and the way in which the cells of the hair are assembled, these two factors then changing what we perceive as the color. Once a gene has mutated, it thereafter acts in a predictable manner.

Let us look at an example from the gene loci known as the C or albino loci. Here the normal gene is for full body color—thus the use of the letter C. At some point in the cat's development, the full color gene mutated to become a gene for no color at all—the albino. However, the normal color gene is the more potent, so that when a cat carrying the albino gene mates with one that has the normal, all the offspring will appear normal but will still be carrying the albino gene, then a proportion of their offspring (25%) will, in fact, be visual albinos. What is more, they will be truebreeding for albinism. Using this example, we can now discuss a number of genetical aspects.

TERMINOLOGY

It is convenient to use

specific genetic words rather than to have to explain things repeatedly—thus allele means the alternative gene of a pair of chromosomes which are the same. Albinism is the allele of normal full color; both are at the same locus on their respective chromosomes. At that locus the cat can carry either the full color gene or it can have the non-color, or albino, gene; it cannot have them both. But chromosomes are paired, so it could carry

devised a shorthand to save space and to make calculations easier. We have seen that C stands for full color, so the letter c in lower case is used to stand for no color or albinism. By using the same letter, we are reminded that albino is the alternative gene at that locus to full color. If we were to

one on one chromosome and one on another—or it could have two of the same kind. As geneticists have developed their own language to explain things, so have they also

use a different letter, things would quickly get out of hand when other genes were included in calculations. The use of a lower case letter denotes that albino is not as potent as full color; it is recessive to it. Full color is thus a dominant gene and albino is a recessive gene. You will see these terms crop up again and again in genetics.

If both of a cat's genes were for full color, this would

chromosomes are always paired, so each gene on each chromosome must be indicated. If the cat carried one of each of the genes, it would have a genotype of *Cc*. This cat would look a normal color, yet the albino gene is there, hidden or masked by the more dominant full color gene. Such a cat would be described as

A champion champagne-colored male Burmese.

be represented by the formula *CC*; if both were for albino, then it would be *cc*. Remember that the

normal split for albino, which can be abbreviated to normal/albino. The color in front of the oblique line is visible, while that behind it is masked. The *CC* cat is a purebreeding cat for its color because that is the only color it can pass on to its offspring; likewise, the albino *cc* is also purebreeding for the same reason. These two are both termed homozygous, indicating that their genes are the same; the zygote from which they were produced was the same color in each of their parents. The *Cc* cat is non-purebreeding, and this is termed being heterozygous for its color, because here its offspring might inherit either a full color gene or one for albino. I should add at this point that true albinism in cats is extremely rare indeed because, by definition, an albino can carry no color pigment at all; it is a pink or red-eyed white; in cats,

most are blue-eyed and not true albinos, because pigment must be present to produce blue or green or orange eyes.

The reader may have noted that it is thus possible to have two types of genotypes in cats which have but a single visual appearance. Both *CC* and *Cc* are normal-looking cats, but they will breed totally differently, so we can now add more genetic terms. Phenotype is the visual look of a cat, while genotype indicates how that look is composed and will thus breed. It is possible for a cat to have a single phenotype, but this may be arrived at by a great number of differing genotypes, so the first hint that all that glitters may not be gold can be seen. A top show winner may have the right combination of genes to be the winner it is, but whether it will pass them on in the right ratio is another story, for it is dependent on random selection.

RANDOM SELECTION

Genes are totally random in the way they are passed from generation to generation—within certain tolerances. If a cat is CC at a given loci, then clearly it can only pass on a C, and likewise if it is cc. However, the Cc cat may pass on C or c, so now there are more possibilities than where purebreeding genes are concerned.

If we look at a few potential matings, these will highlight the very basics of heredity. Firstly, you will remember it was stated that, in the germ cells, only one of a pair of chromosomes exists due to the way in which the germ cells are formed. This means that only one gene of an alternative pair can be passed to the offspring; thus it will receive one for that locus, thus feature, from each parent. The question of dominance or recession does not affect matters, as each gene has an equal chance of being passed on.

If a cat which is CC is mated to one of cc genotype, all of the young will be normal in color, but now it can be seen why this is so. The CC can only pass on a C gene and the cc only a c; there is no other possibility, so the

A champion champagne-colored
Burmese.

	c	c
C	Cc	Cc
C	Cc	Cc

	C	c
C	CC	Cc
C	CC	Cc

kittens *must* have a genotype of Cc, and as normal is dominant to albino, they will be normal in appearance but split for albino.

If one of these youngsters is mated to the CC parent, then the equation will read $CC \times Cc = CC, Cc, CC, Cc$. Once again, all of the kittens produced will be normal in appearance, but now half of them are purebreeding for normal, the other half being normal/albino. There is no way of telling which are which without a series of test matings, which could be costly in terms of the number of kittens being produced before a definite decision could be reached about the genetic state of the individual.

If a Cc cat is paired to a cc, then the equation will read $Cc \times cc = Cc, Cc, cc, cc$. This translates to 50% normal/albinos and 50% albinos, but in this instance the purebreeding

	C	c
c	Cc	cc
c	Cc	cc

types *cc* are visually apparent as such, where the purebreeding *CC* individuals were not. This shows that a dominant gene can express itself if only present in single quantity, but a recessive *must* be present in double dose before it becomes apparent. Such a mating would also highlight another aspect—can you spot what this is? In the answer lies the basis of test matings. A normal cat was mated to an albino and produced albino offspring. The only way this is possible is if the normal itself also carried the albino gene. To be visually albino, the cat must have both its genes for this "color," but we know that the albino parent can only pass on one albino gene, so the other must have come from the other parent, as, in fact, was the case. Thus if you wish to test for the state of a potentially split individual, it must be paired to a recessive, and the appearance of just one of the recessives in a litter confirms the parent was a heterozygous animal, not homozygous for that particular feature. However, the non-appearance of an albino does not, *ipso facto*, establish that the parent must be purebreeding, and this is because of the random nature of chance.

In each of the equations used as examples, every potential combination of the genes was made between the two parents. This establishes the potential recombinations and their relative ratio to each other, but it does not follow that this equates the actual kittens that will be born. If you flip a coin, you know for certain that there are only two possible ways it can land—heads or tails—but if you flip it twice or three times, it may land heads on each occasion; but that does not indicate it is therefore a double-headed penny. Enough flips and the tail will land face up, and if you continue flipping, the predicated

ratio of 50% heads and tails will become more accurate the more times you flip. Genetics works on exactly the same basis in terms of probabilities. However, if an albino did not turn up in two or three litters of four or five kittens using the same parents, then the probability is indeed that the normal parent was in fact pure for its color. If 12 heads turned up on successive coin flips, then the probability is moving strongly towards the fact that it is, in fact, a double-headed penny.

We will complete the series of matings to explore each of the possibles using just two contrasting genes. If Cc and Cc parents are paired, the equation will be Cc x $Cc = CC$, Cc, cC, and cc.

This color of a Burmese might not be acceptable in some places. Often called "lilac," the color is not listed in the CFA standard, but the standards of most other countries do list lilac.

This thus produces theoretical expectations of 25% purebreeding normals, 50% non-purebreeding normals and 25% pure albino. This ratio of 1:2:1 is very common in breeding, though visually, 75% of the offspring are normal in their color.

SERIES OF MUTATIONS

Once a mutation has appeared at a given locus, it is quite possible that a further mutation may appear at that locus, and when this happens, geneticists arrange the mutations in a series based on their known powers of expression. At the C locus there are known to be a number of mutant genes, but only four are known in cats, and in order of dominance are as follows:

C

= Full color (black and orange, at full strength)

cb

= Burmese (black diluted to brown, orange to yellow)

cs

= Siamese (the points are dark but the body color is diluted to off-white or pale sepia)

ca

= Blue-eyed white (no pigment in coat, thus pure white)

c

= Albino (no pigment at all—the red of the eyes is reflection of the blood in the tissue)

The C gene is totally dominant to each of its alleles, but the others are only partially dominant to each other. Do remember that a cat can carry only one of these genes at that locus on a chromosome, so that a Burmese is cbcb genotype. If it is paired to a Siamese, then the result will be cbcs and, as Burmese color is only partially dominant to Siamese, the appearance is that of a light Burmese (known in the USA as the Tonkinese).

OTHER COAT COLOR LOCI

You may be wondering where the other Burmese coat colors come from, given that only brown (seal or sable) appears to be featured at the albino locus. We have considered only one locus in order to explain how genes are inherited, but color is controlled by about six different loci in the cat, and each of these has its effect on color. Space does not permit an in-depth study of each locus, and for a greater understanding of color transmission, the reader is advised to acquire one of the books specifically written on feline genetics.

If you have been able to understand the basics so far discussed, then from this you will be able to follow progressively more detailed text on a build-up basis. For example, the blue Burmese has the formula *aaB-cbcbdd*, and while this may appear rather daunting to the beginner, it is actually not so because each gene

locus can be interpreted as a separate unit. The *aa* means that at the agouti locus, the Burmese carries the gene for non-agouti. The *B-* means that the pigment of the hair is black and, as it is dominant, needs to be present only in single form to show itself; the - means that the genotype may thus be *BB* or *Bb*. We have already discussed the situation at the albino or *c* locus which has the effect of diluting the black color. Finally, *dd* is also a dilution gene, being the allele of *D*, which produces dense pigment, thus *d* dilutes the brown to become blue.

PRACTICAL APPLICATION

From what has been discussed thus far, it will

be appreciated that if a blue Burmese is mated with a blue Burmese, then only blue Burmese will result because in each case the genes at the various loci are pure or homozygous.

However, the one gene that may be the exception to this statement is at the *B* locus, which may or

The Tonkinese to the left is dark in color; the Tonkinese to the right is lighter in color. With a proper understanding of genetics...and the genetic makeup of your breeding stock, you might be able to predict the outcome of a particular crossing. This is especially true of coat and eye color. Tonkinese were created by crossing Burmese with Siamese. Owner, S.L. and M.S. Reams.

may not be purebreeding. If one parent is pure for this and the other is heterozygous, then the kittens will all be blue, but 50% of them will be blue split for lilac. In using formula for calculating results, we can shorten matters by calculating out only the situations where the genes are not pure from both parents for that feature. Let us consider mating a chocolate, which carries the dilution gene, to a lilac. The full formula for the mating would be *aabbcbcbDd* x *aabbcbcbdd*, but it can be seen that the only difference between the chocolate *Dd* and the lilac *dd* is in the degree of dilution, for in all other genes both parents can pass on only the same genotypes, so only one combination of them is possible, plus the variables of the dilution factor. This latter combination is the same as used in our normal/albino x albino examples, so the results will be *Dd* x *dd* = *Dd, Dd, dd, dd*; translated, this is 50% chocolates split for lilac and 50% lilacs. Were the chocolate to be purebreeding, *DD* then mated to a lilac could only result in one genotype, which would be *Dd*, so all the kittens would only be visually chocolate, but all would carry the dilution gene for lilac.

The genetic formulas for the other colors not already discussed are as follows:

Brown—*aaB-$c^b c^b$D-*
Red—*$c^b c^b$D-O* (male) and
   D-OO (female)
Tortie—*aaB-$c^b c^b$D-Oo*

Blue cream—$aaB\text{-}c^bc^ddOo$
Chocolate tortie—
    $aabbc^bc^bD\text{-}Oo$
Lilac Tortie—$aabbc^bc^bddOo$

In the USA the chocolate is better known as the champagne, while the lilac is often referred to as the platinum. It is likely that the pigment cells for color are thermo-sensitive, by which is meant that the darker points become darker the colder the climate is, and this should not be confused with paling due to gene action. This characteristic is by no means specific to the Burmese, or indeed to cats, as it is exhibited in other pets, such as rabbits and mice, where the Siamese pattern is called Himalayan. This fact is interesting and illustrates another aspect of genetics—you do not need to refer to genetics only as applied to Burmese, or even cats, when making further study, because mammalian genetics clearly have a common root. There are more color varieties in mice than in any other pets, so that study of their genetics is worthwhile because it may have direct interest to the future situation in felines.

SEX LINKAGE

In most aspects of color, the color is totally independent of the sex of the cat, but sometimes it may be linked to the gender, as in the case of the red, which genetically is known as orange. It has been seen that, in discussion so far, the chromosome pairs are the same, but in the case of the sex chromosomes, this is not so. One, called the Y, is much shorter than its opposite chromosome, known as the X. In cats, a male has a genotype of XY while the female is XX. The X chromosome can carry color but the Y chromosome is largely concerned with sexual differences and does not carry color, as it has no opposing axis segment to that of the X.

This means that a male can carry orange O, or its allele o, non-orange. A female, having two X chromosomes, can carry two genes for O; thus she would be OO, which is technically yellow, but this covers variation from red to pale cream. She might also be Oo, and this

is the interesting color we know as tortoiseshell, where the two genes both manifest themselves on differing parts of the body at the same time. The O produces the red (or orange) color, while the o (non-orange) results in any other colors but those of the yellow range.

Finally, she may be oo, which simply means she is any other color but yellow. Because tortoiseshell is a heterozygote Oo, it is not possible, in theory, to have tortoiseshell males, though they do in fact exist as a result of genetic

Facing Page: This Burmese has been called many things in terms of its color. Lilac, Malayan, grey and light are all adjectives that have been used in Europe to describe this color variation.

mix-ups. Such males have the rare genotype of *XOXoY*. They are invariably sterile, however.

Calculations involving sex-linked genes are done in the normal manner, but you must always keep track of the sex involved, so it is useful to include the sex chromosomes in calculations. As an example, let us mate a red male with a tortie female, which will have the

Genetic characters that are variable in Burmese are eye color, fur color and shape of face. You must know something about cat genetics in order to understand the parameters and variables.

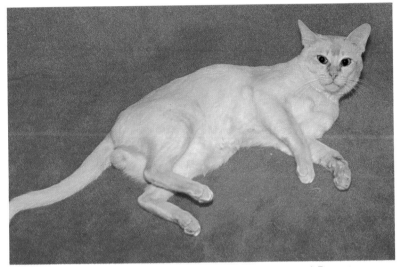

Coat color is the most simple characteristic in the study of Burmese genetics. If you have two cats of this color, chances are that the offspring will also have this same color because this color is recessive for Burmese.

following equation:

$XOY \times XOXo = XOXO$
$XOXo \; XOY \; XoY$

Translating this will produce the following theoretical expectations: 25% red females, 25% tortie females, 25% red males, 25% non-red males (i.e., brown or other color).

Once again, the laws of chance are involved, so you have a one-in-four chance that each variety will turn up, and a 50:50 chance that reds will appear, but this is based over large numbers, and in any one litter the actual ratios may fluctuate.

In all genetic calculations, always ensure that you take account of every potential permutation of the genes.

with *XO* or *Xo*, thus giving us the full permutations. Of course, if more than one pair of genes were being calculated for, then the potential permutations begin to rise quite

This lovely Burmese may be heterozygous (genetically mixed up) and thus an undependable breeder, or it may be genetically pure (homozygous) and, when bred with another homozygous Burmese, can have fairly predictable offspring. Owner, Diane Quaas-Lopez.

In the example just given, *XO* could combine with *XO* or *Xo* of the opposing chromosome, and likewise *Y* could combine

dramatically, so that if three genes are being considered, together with one allele for each, then there are 64 permutations,

Mature Burmese males sometimes develop a fullness in the cheek area. Most Burmese admirers prefer the more triangular and lean look.

while for four pairs the number of permutations rises to 256. It will be appreciated that it is hardly practical to calculate for numerous genes, because the numbers of litters needed to obtain all of the phenotypes would be impossible to breed.

SEX DETERMINATION

It has been stated that the sexes are *XX* (female) and *XY* (male), and if you consider the permutations of these, they work out at exactly 50/50 of each, so this is the theoretical likelihood to be found in litters. Some litters will have a bias one way, others the other, but over any number of litters, the number of males to females will be about even.

BREEDING FOR TYPE

In breeding for color, we have been dealing with major genes, but where breed type is concerned, the situation is different, and here continuous variation is the factor that is most evident. It is very difficult to isolate the various components of a cat's body, from a genetic viewpoint, because these may be linked with other features, and we do not know whether that feature is better in the pure or impure state. Only when a gene

Facing page: Breeding for type is extremely difficult for the novice. This lovely Burmese could be typical (that's where the word "type" comes from), and this type could be bred for, if that is your ideal for a Burmese. Owner, Diane Quaas-Lopez.

mutates in a major way are we able to notice its effect, and then selectively breed for that feature if it is deemed desirable. This, however, has not happened in cats other than in color or hair length and composition.

Given this fact, then it is a case of trying to retain desired features while trying to remove, by selection, non-desired features. We must assume that if a given cat looks impressive, this is because the desirable features are dominant to the non-desired features; we must also assume that they are better in the homozygous state than in the heterozygous state, and, further, we must assume that what we consider to be desirable features are not in any way linked to

either internal problems or undesirable physical features or abnormalities. It will be appreciated that we are making a great number of presumptions, and it is known that we are clearly wrong in some of these—which places more importance on the need to be selective and to place greater attention on such matters as breeding vigor and resistance to disease. It is of no benefit to the breed as a whole if trends produce superior cats on the one side but with a progressively higher number of abnormalities and reduced vigor on the other. The Burmese breed itself is the result of selective inbreeding in order to retain given features while removing the undesirable ones, so

It's fine to breed Burmese according to the standard, but keep in mind that breeding for health, personality and temperament is also of great importance.

clearly a policy in which certain genes are retained is the pathway to improving a breeder's strain. Given continuous variation, or polygenic action, then the object is to build up the number of plus genes working towards improvement of a feature while reducing the minus genes that detract from that feature. To achieve this, it would follow that it is not wise to breed in a haphazard manner using unrelated animals, because this will involve using stock whose genotype we know little or nothing about. If we stay within family lines, then it is likely, by rigid selection, that we will steadily increase the percentage of the desired genes and correspondingly reduce the number of undesirables.

Examination of any really well-established line of Burmese cats will reveal that this is the best way to steadily improve the overall quality of litters, though it does not follow that it will automatically produce top winners; but it produces consistency because it creates a more homozygous pool of genes. Much thus depends upon how good the key cats are on which one is developing a line. You will appreciate, however, that if one is fixing in desired points, it is likely that faults will also become more fixed, simply because, in the initial stages of breeding, the faults will be hidden or only apparent now and

All cats love to chase small, moving objects. This was a toy mouse at the end of a fishing line. It was dangled until it tormented the poor Burmese. But the cat had its revenge! With a lightening-fast swat it captured the toy mouse...only to be disappointed that it was made of soft cotton. Owner, Diane Quaas-Lopez.

then as double recessives. The more we inbreed, the greater the chance of the recessives coming together so that inbreeding will show up the faults in our stock. This has obvious merit but carries the singular problem that, once the fault has become established, then to remove it means moving out of our genetic line to introduce a cat that does not suffer with the fault. However, in so doing, much of the good work done on other features may be undone, because the introduced cat may not be as pure for the feature that our stock excels in.

If things were easy, everyone would be breeding super Burmese, and it is these continual problems that serve to separate the top breeders from those less capable. The general approach should therefore be to commence your breeding operations with cats that are from a strain that shows a certain degree of duplication in its line; indeed, this would be a prerequisite to justify the tag "a strain." Having commenced with a given line of breeding, stay within that line as long as possible and breed only with the very best of your stock. To do this, you can grade youngsters against

Facing page: The European standard for Burmese may differ substantially from the English/American ideal. This is a German champion. It has a completely different appearance than that of the more familiar English/American Burmese.

a point system for numerous features. To improve on this, you place the features in the order you believe to be the most important, and then give these a value. You may consider the heads of your cats to need improving, so you rate this as eight points, compared with the breeding vigor, which is given seven; in turn, feet may rate six points and color five points, and so on. Total scores are thus based on multiplying the rating by the score out of five or ten, or whatever number of points you allocate to each feature (which is scored by the same number of points). If a kitten had an especially good head compared to your average stock, then it might gain seven out of

ten, which is then multiplied by eight to give 56 points. When all the scores are worked out for each kitten, this total score system will show the overall best kittens to retain. You will find that, by having a coefficient included, a kitten which may not have scored so well out of ten, feature for feature, stands out clearly, when total score is considered, because of the high value you place on head quality at that time. The coefficients will clearly change once you

Facing page: when trying to breed a better Burmese, you should not be emotional. Consider each characteristic of your cat including its coat color, head, feet, etc. Make a value judgment and then go for it, selecting the parents which best display your optimum dream cat. Owner, Diane Quaas-Lopez.

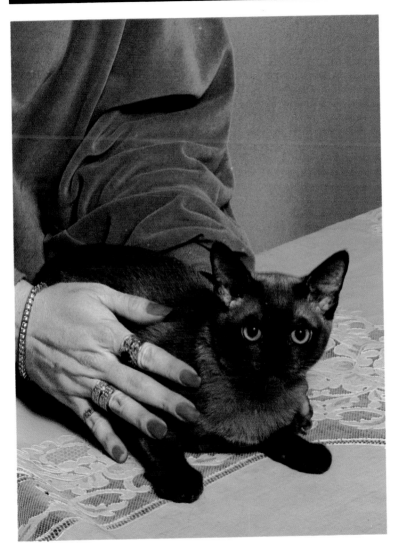

have obtained the sort of heads you want—by which time another feature might need improving, and on it goes.

There are indeed many ways you can evaluate stock, but in each case they are only as good as your own ability to critically apply judgments. Whenever using a stud, always do as much checking as you can

Burmese should be kept clean and parasite-free at all times. Your local pet shop will have sprays, dips, shampoos (both wet and dry), powders and patent remedies for washing, bathing, de-fleaing and grooming your cat's beautiful coat. In most cases, your Burmese will enjoy the attention it is getting. Owner, Diane Quaas-Lopez.

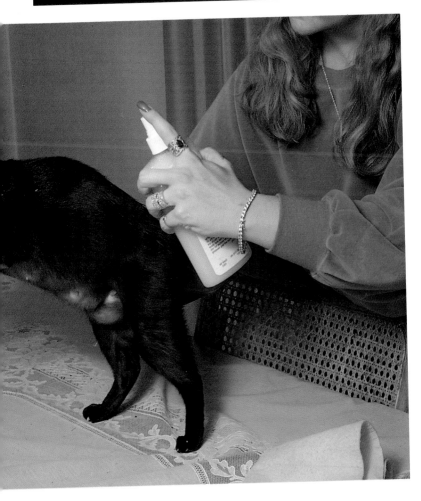

to find out if it has a good record of passing on the features which you are essentially using it for. If it fails to produce the desired results, it is usually better to use a different stud in the future rather than persist, pending exploring the stud's genetic potential. Sometimes this latter method can pay good dividends, which only goes to show that there are indeed many ways each breeder can tackle a problem, yet arrive at the same objective: improving one's stock over any given

Burmese are inquisitive, sure-footed, attentive pets. They require love and attention. Be careful when your cat is ready for breeding as any available male will serve the purpose.

Burmese are friendly, easily trained cats. In many cases they are very affectionate, especially when it gets close to breeding time. Cat owned by Mrs. Haake.

span of time.

Even if you become only an occasional breeder, you will find that a study of genetics can become quite fascinating, because, if nothing else, it will teach you to apply caution. You will be aware of the ways genes are transmitted and can hide faults for a number of generations. At best, you will become hooked on the subject as, block by block, you build onto your basic knowledge of the subject.

Exhibition

Exhibiting Burmese is a really interesting aspect of cat owning and is a logical conclusion to breeding. Competing with other breeders in the show world will reveal just how successful your breeding is. You will be getting the opinion of experts as to the quality of your stock, as compared with your own

Most house cats, especially Burmese, must have their claws clipped on a regular basis. This is especially true if you intend to show your Burmese. Pet shops sell special tools for cutting your cat's claws.

view of things, which is reflected in the cats you produce. However, exhibiting is time consuming and can be costly, so it is not an area you should rush into without first doing a little preparatory research.

The first thing to do is to visit a number of shows in your area, both large and small ones if possible, as they differ considerably in both the quality of cats to be seen and in the general atmosphere of the occasion. Study the prize-winners, for these are the cats yours must compete with, and you must be honest in appraising their virtues and your own stock's faults. Exhibitors are a friendly bunch, on the whole, and are always willing to offer the novice advice on how to go about entering the shows in your area, when the forthcoming shows will be held, and what the general regulations are. It will certainly be beneficial to join your area cat society, and it will be obligatory to have your cat registered with either the national ruling body (UK) or with one of the many registration associations in your country (USA and Australia). In the following text, the comments made are necessarily of a rather general view; this is because the rules of exhibition differ from country to country, and even association to association, so you are recommended to check out details of showing from your registration body.

TYPES OF SHOWS

Basically, shows are graded by the size of their normal entries, so that the largest exhibitions are the championship shows, which may be all-breed affairs or they may be

Facing page: Your house cat, being an aristocratic Burmese, can bring you a lot of extra pleasure if you decide to enter it into a cat show. Cat people are, by their very nature, friendly and cooperative. They'll usually be very happy to help you get started. Join your local cat club and meet new friends with a common interest.

restricted to a single breed if the breed is numerically popular. At such events, the quality of the cats entered is normally extremely high and the prize-winners represent the very cream of cats at that point in time. Such shows are held in major cities and attract many entries, as well as thousands of visitors, and they may be spread over two or three days. At these shows, the coveted challenge certificates are gained in the UK, or valuable points in the USA, which contribute toward the title of champion. In the champions class, wins then go toward the title of Grand Champion for whole cats, or for Grand Premiers in the case of altered cats (the

equivalent to a champion in an altered cat being known as a premier cat).

The next level of shows are those which do not offer challenge certificates, and these are called sanction shows. They are not so large, but they otherwise follow the same procedures as the championship shows. Competition is still fierce but slightly less so than at the really big shows, as breeders do not travel quite such great distances to attend them. The

Facing page: There is nothing that can be overlooked in grooming your Burmese for the upcoming cat show. Pay particular attention to the cat's ears, as this important point is often overlooked by beginners but never overlooked by judges. Owner, Diane Quaas-Lopez.

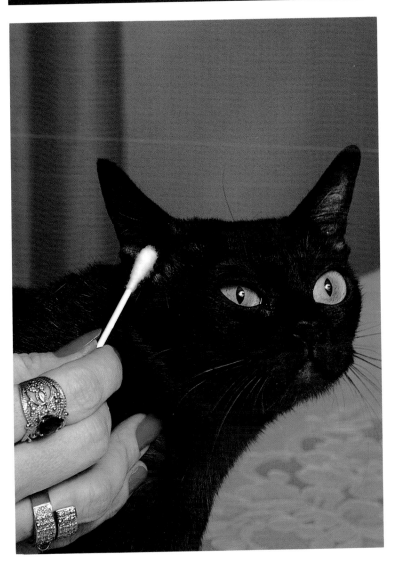

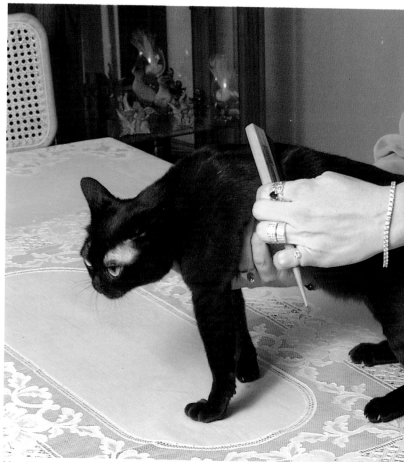

Your local pet shop will have special grooming tools with which you can keep your Burmese in tip-top condition at all times. Many Burmese enjoy the grooming experience. Owner, Diane Quaas-Lopez.

smallest shows are known as exemption shows, and here the atmosphere is much less charged, so they are very informal and the rules are usually more relaxed than at the bigger exhibitions. This does not imply that they are not important within the overall exhibition structure; indeed, for many people they may well be the sort of shows they support, as they are very local, and often the really big winners will not be competing, so they are excellent both for novice owners and cats of similar standing.

CLASSES

The most important class at a major show is that known as the open, as it is from this that the major winners emerge to compete for the very top awards, including that for the Best in Show. There are then many side classes which may be for novice cats (those which have not won prizes), maidens, debutante, best groomed, bred by exhibitor, or bred in the state of the show venue, and so on. Most shows also include childrens' classes, as the organizers are aware that today's youngsters are tomorrow's champion breeders. There are also classes for non-pedigreed pet cats, and a number of people who have won in these have then gone on to become pedigreed cat owners. There is thus ample choice of classes and, apart from the awards given for these, there may well be additional prizes offered where a club sponsors a class, in which case you become eligible, providing you are a paid up member of that club. The classes are, of course, divided according to the breeds—exactly how many classes being determined by the anticipated number of entrants. Clearly, at the smaller shows you may not always find a classification for Burmese, who would thus be shown as Foreign Shorthairs. Should you win in your breed class, then you will go on to compete with other

Facing page: This is a lovely house pet. It may not be champion quality, but it can be shown, as most cat shows have classes for non-pedigreed cats. Show your cat...it's great fun and a great experience.

breeds for the honor of the Best in Show. Direct comparison between breeds obviously cannot be done, so for this award the judge must decide if your Burmese is a better example of the breed than someone else's Siamese, or Longhair, is of theirs. Although the Best in Show award is a very popular spectacle as far as the public is concerned, it is the Best of Breed that is really the one that counts, because here you will have gained the prize

Grooming your Burmese for the first cat show of its life is very important as a training experience. It is an experience for both you and the cat. You should get instructions from a successful Burmese groomer. Owner, Diane Quaas-Lopez.

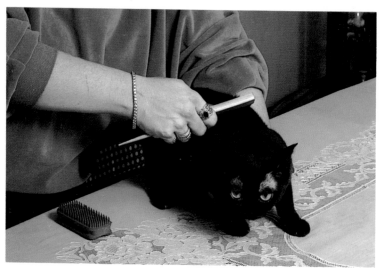

Age requirements for showing vary from country to country. Officially, a kitten is a kitten until it is nine months old in the UK, or eight months old in the USA. Owner, Diane Quaas-Lopez.

under a specialist Burmese judge as compared with the person who is judging sections, usually an all-rounder judge.

SHOW AGE

In the UK, a kitten remains as such until it reaches the age of nine months, after which it must be entered into adult classes; in the USA, it is eight months of age. Kitten classes may be all embracing or they may be divided further, such as three to five months and five to nine months, depending on the size of the show. In Australia, some exhibitions will allow under 12-week-old kittens to be shown, but this is not possible in the UK or the USA.

JUDGING

In the UK, the procedure is that, while judging is being done, the exhibitors are requested to leave the venue, and only when judging has been completed are they and the public allowed to enter the hall. If there is a gallery to the venue, then exhibitors may be allowed to use this to observe matters. The judges go around to each show pen in turn and examine the cats carefully before placing the awards on the appropriate show pens. In this task they have a steward to assist them to remove and replace the cats to their pens while they make suitable judging notes.

In the USA, matters are different, and the whole show is geared to provide a more colorful and exciting spectacle. The cats are transferred from their pens to pens near the judge, and then each cat is assessed in turn for each class so arranged. The public and exhibitors are allowed to watch everything, and a good judge can really build up excitement as he or she moves up and down the line of cats examined before finally placing the winner's rosette on the pen. At a really big show,

Facing page: A beautiful example of a sable Burmese.

and for the top awards, many an owner is speechless upon gaining the major honor.

Attempts were made at the beginning of the century to show cats just as dogs are shown, that is, on a lead in a show ring. Can you just imagine the scene of two un-neutered toms in close proximity to each other! Needless to say, after many a fight, the idea was dropped, and thereafter cats were always kept in totally enclosed wire show pens.

In the UK, the show pens are fitted out in white—bowl and blanket—but in the USA, the pens are decorated to suit your own taste, so that beautiful side curtains and colorful pillows are used to create a complementary

Facing page: Cat shows have been around for almost 100 years...and each year they become better attended. The quality of the Burmese, too, gets better as more specimens obviously produce better cats. Cat shows are always sponsored by someone, some club or some national interest. These sponsoring bodies make up rules. These rules are often the result of bitter experiences. In the UK, for example, the judges work without the owners being present. In the USA, things are completely different. The judging takes place in the open, with the public, the owners, and the competitors all watching what is going on. In the UK, all the pens are the same, painted white. In the USA, you can decorate your show pen any way you desire. Australia, South Africa, and New Zealand have rules varying between the rules of the UK and the USA. Owner, Diane Quaas-Lopez.

backdrop to match the cats. The sense of occasion has always been a strong point with Americans,

and this is reflected in cat shows, which are most enjoyable to visit. Britain, by direct comparison, tends to be more reserved and conservative in the way it approaches things, but the quality of the cats is quite outstanding at times. Australia represents a good half-way house, having such long links with the UK yet expressing identity in true Australian style. Australians do have problems, however, in that, with such vast distances to travel between states, they cannot attract the enormous entries seen in the USA and UK, and this must affect the strength of the competition available.

In the UK it is customary for the judges to wear white overalls, whereas in the USA the judges often compete with the pens, insomuch as they will dress for the occasion in colorful and quite immaculate clothes. It is also quite normal for an American judge to provide a commentary while judging, whereas in the UK it is a case of reading the judges' critique in the specialist press to see what they thought of an exhibit—unless the judge has a little free time when he/she will often discuss the merits and faults of your cat with you.

SHOW ENTRY

Once a show date is announced, schedules are available from the secretary of the show. These explain the rules and also indicate the

Cat shows are always well attended. Even local shows have hundreds of entries most of the time. Showing your cat can be very enlightening. Not only do you learn a lot about Burmese, but you get to meet some very nice people. You should consider showing your Burmese if it is of sufficiently good quality.

various classes scheduled. These must be filled in with care, because an incorrect entry will result in disqualification. The appropriate fee is then returned with the entry, and this should all be done as soon as possible, for it takes some weeks to prepare catalogs and have the correct number of show pens available. The schedule will indicate last date of entry.

Shortly before the show date, you will receive your show pen label together with a vetting-in card, which must be presented to the vet, and you will receive your own exhibitors' pass. On arrival at the show, all cats are checked to see they are in healthy condition; this is a wise precaution in everyone's interests. This attended to, you can then locate your pen number, which will be together with other Burmese owners; in the USA, cats are not penned by breed, so you may apply to be near friends even if they have a different breed. The first thing to do is to settle the cat down with its blanket, water supply and give it a final "polish," so it looks at its best for the judge. Feeding is not allowed until after judging, but water must be available for the exhibits throughout the show.

Apart from the needs of the cat, you should remember to take a flask of tea or coffee for yourself, plus a packed lunch, because often there are long queues for these, especially at the larger shows which attract many onlookers. Always allow plenty of travelling time to the show location, because sometimes you may have to drive quite a way to find suitable parking for your car. You must, of course, transport your cat in a carrying basket, as it is not allowed to take a cat into a show venue without one. It is also illegal to have a cat loose in a car in the UK unless a second person is in the car to hold the animal; this of course applies to a moving vehicle, not to one that is stationary.

AFTER THE SHOW

When you return from a show, it is wise to keep exhibition cats away from others, at least for a few days, just to be sure they have not by chance picked up an illness while at the show. Obviously, with so many cats together in a venue, this is a possibility in spite of the precautions taken to prevent it. This factor you must consider before becoming an exhibitor. It is wise to wash all of your cat's

blankets after each show, and do remember to place vaccination certificates back in a safe place until needed again.

The show world is a social scene of its own, and you are sure to make many new friends at exhibitions, and certainly your knowledge of Burmese will widen as a result of participation. Of course, there are many breeders who rarely, if ever, exhibit, yet are frequent show goers so they can keep abreast of what is winning, old friends and the general gossip of the show circuit. At shows, you will also find trade stands which carry every possible feline item.

Health Matters

Burmese are hardy cats so that, provided with a well-balanced diet, it is likely they will suffer only from the sort of routine ailments we all get in life: colds, coughs, minor skin problems, cuts and bruises. There are, of course, a great number of serious diseases cats may contract, but these can be treated only by your

Burmese are intelligent, beautiful, hardy and tough cats. They always look alert, with bright eyes and a shiny coat. When these health signs are missing, your cat may be ill.

veterinarian, so cataloging them has little practical benefit to the average owner, who needs to know how to cope with the everyday type of problems that could occur. This chapter will look at general symptoms to major problems and then detail common ailments.

CLINICAL SYMPTOMS

The most usual sign that a cat is beginning to feel ill is when it loses interest in its food; this may or may not be accompanied by diarrhea. It will appear listless and will spend more time curled up asleep. If things get worse, then its third eyelid or haw will become visible across the bottom of the eye, there may be a nasal discharge, and the

If your Burmese ceases regular daily activities such as grooming, it could be a sign that he is not feeling up to par.

eyes may weep. As an illness takes greater hold, the urine or feces may contain blood and will have a very foul odor. The cat will become more reclusive, spending long periods asleep. It may vomit, have difficulty in breathing (when you will hear a wheezing sound), and if blood is seen in the vomit, then things are getting very bad.

These various symptoms cover just about every major illness, so you will appreciate that home diagnosis of an illness is a very unwise thing to attempt. The general rule you should apply is that if a minor problem has not cleared up, or is not showing signs of so doing within 48 hours, then you must consult your veterinarian.

Do remember that while this may sometimes appear premature, the sooner a vet can examine your cat the more easily it can be treated, thus halting the advancement of the illness. In many cases, the cause of a problem can be determined only by microscopy of the feces or of blood samples. Thus, it is always useful if you can have samples of feces or vomit available for your veterinarian.

The normal temperature of a cat is in the range of 38.6°C (101.5°F), and this may vary slightly depending on the climate, the individual cat and its state at the time its temperature is taken (if it has been playing or running as compared with sleeping).

If the reading is over 39°C (102.2°F), then this may be considered feverish. What has happened is that the cat's internal regulator has not switched on, so heat, thus energy, is being retained by the body to combat the illness. As the illness reaches and passes its peak, the thermo-regulator starts to work, and in order to reduce body temperature the animal sweats or pants, thus creating surface evaporation which reduces the temperature, and the cat starts to get better.

To take your cat's temperature, you will need a clinical thermometer with a bulbous end to it. Before use it should be given a sharp shake so that the mercury is down to the bulb end. Wipe the thermometer with a suitable lubricant (vegetable oil or something similar), and then place it into the cat's anus to a length just short of about 2.5cm (1 in). Tilt it slightly so it is pressing against the anal wall and hold it in position for about 60 seconds, when you can withdraw it and read off the temperature. You will find it easier to do this if somebody is helping you by securing the cat, which will not otherwise be found very cooperative.

ISOLATION

Once you have decided that your cat is definitely off-color, it should be isolated pending advice or treatment by the veterinarian. When an illness has been confirmed, the isolation must be maintained until the ailment has been cured; otherwise the health of your other cats is placed at risk.

A hospital cage can be very useful at such times, and this can be put together without too much problem, especially if you already have a large dog crate. Put a clean blanket in it so the cat will be comfortable. The crate must then be placed into a warm spot, where a constant temperature can be maintained and where there is no risk of a draft. It is certainly worthwhile to purchase an infrared lamp, which can be suspended at a suitable height above the crate. Place it at one end so that the cat can move away from the hottest part at its convenience, as the last thing you want to do is to induce stress in the animal, as this will be counter-productive in terms of improving the condition being treated.

Even better is to have a thermostat wired into the infrared's circuit, and in this way you are assured of a controlled temperature. Obviously the cat should be placed where it is quiet and where the lights are not especially bright. A water dish should be available at all times; the extra heat will induce thirst and it may be possible to add medicaments to the water (though the range is actually limited because many have a short life in water, and one cannot be

Ping's Caprice of Sambur, a ten-month old female Burmese owned by Mr. and Mrs. L.D. Sample.

sure how much the cat will drink—so dosing is unreliable). Once a cat has recovered from an illness, its room temperature must be reduced over a few days so that it is acclimatized back to the outside temperature.

DIGESTIVE PROBLEMS

The most common minor problems likely to befall your Burmese in terms of digestion will be either diarrhea or its opposite, constipation. Far less likely will be hairballs. In the case of diarrhea, reduce the protein content of the diet and increase the roughage, such as cereals; do not withhold water. A change in diet may cause diarrhea, though technically it is not that but merely rather loose feces. True diarrhea is associated with many conditions of the digestive organs, so if it persists, it must be referred to your vet. Constipation may be created by a blockage, as with hairballs, or it may be the result of a diet lacking moist content, or simply through lack of exercise. Add bran or something similar to the diet to increase roughage; giving medicinal liquid paraffin may also alleviate the condition. A few drops of cod liver oil on the food may also help matters. Hairballs are more a problem with longhaired cats that ingest hairs as they groom themselves; the hairs form balls in the stomach and prevent the onward movement of food. If your Burmese is groomed regularly you will not have this problem, so the blockage would have another cause which must be referred to a veterinarian.

EXTERNAL PARASITES

The most common parasite on a cat's skin will be fleas. These tiny arthropods are easily seen running in the hairs, but are less likely to be noticed in the dark-colored varieties of Burmese. They live by sucking the blood of their host, and infestations can create anemia as well as secondary problems resulting from any germs the fleas are carrying and as a result of scratches the cat makes in its attempt to rid itself of the pests. Lice are grayish creatures that move much more slowly through the fur but also live on the blood of the host. Regular inspection of the coat will reveal them, and they are most likely to be found during the warmer months of the

Fleas run around on the skin of the Burmese, between the hairs, sucking blood until they are fairly bursting. They breed rapidly and can soon make a cat's life miserable unless they are treated with flea spray (available at most pet shops).

year. Treatment is simple and effective by sprays from your pet dealer or vet. Repeat treatment is required, according to instructions on the label, and this is to kill eggs that may hatch after the first treatment. Of course, all bedding must also be treated and, after heavy infestations, it is better burnt.

Ticks may be found on your cats, especially if you live in rural districts. They bury their headparts into the cat and do not move but fill themselves with blood before falling off. Do not just pull them off with tweezers, as their mandibles will remain and may create abscesses. Dab them with alcohol, methyl, etc. so they relax their hold; concentrated salt solutions will also induce this. They may then be removed; check that the wound left is clean and treat this with an antiseptic.

INTERNAL PARASITES

There are a large number of worms that may live in a cat's body, but the ones that create most problems are roundworms, tapeworms, hookworms and threadworms. In all cases, they do not suck blood but may live on the partly digested food within the alimentary tract. The eggs of the various worms are released from the cat via the feces, and these may be directly eaten by other cats or may be ingested via other hosts, such as mice, rats and so forth; in this way the life cycle is continued.

Cats suffering from worms will be anemic, usually have diarrhea, which may be blood-streaked, and they may vomit. Often, as infestation builds up, they increase their appetite, but then this reverses and they become disinterested in their food. They may become (especially kittens) potbellied. In all cases, your veterinarian will prescribe suitable treatments.

Pregnant queens should be de-wormed prior to mating, and regular worming twice per year is a sound precaution in all cats. Hygiene is most important, and any worms voided should be burnt. Always maintain maximum personal hygiene by washing your hands after cleaning up any feline feces; better still, use rubber gloves or disposable medical gloves—this is especially important for pregnant women.

There are other internal parasites such as flukes, heartworms, and unicellular organisms, all of which produce similar symptoms of diarrhea, vomiting and general loss of condition. If any parasitic cause is suspected, take samples of the feces to your vet, who will be able to identify the culprit and even do egg counts in order to establish relative degree of infestation. Worms will not be a problem if you cook all meats correctly and maintain hygiene. Internal parasites all respond to modern veterinary treatment.

WOUNDS AND STINGS

Being very athletic, Burmese manage to avoid situations where serious wounds might be caused, so wounds will tend to be of a minor nature—maybe resulting from fights with other cats. In such cases, they need only be carefully wiped clean and then treated with a suitable antiseptic cream and checked daily to see that they heal.

Deep wounds will need stitches, so you should first stem the blood flow as best you can with lint and a pressure bandage. Restrict the cat's movements, if necessary, by wrapping it in a bath towel or blanket, and rush it to the veterinarian. Do not place very tight bandages on for long periods, as these will restrict blood flow and may create subsequent problems; periodically loosen tourniquets.

Bee, wasp and other insect stings will usually be the result of a cat attempting to bite the insect, so these stings are normally found in the mouth parts. The saying "once bitten twice shy" could be applied to stings, and, once stung, cats have a healthy respect for any creature even resembling a bee. However, that first sting may swell inside the mouth and restrict breathing, so immediate veterinary attention is required, as it is most unlikely the cat will allow you to inspect the mouth—let alone remove the stinger (wasps do not leave their stingers

This Burmese is following the flight of a bee. It has had the bad experience of once catching a bee in flight. It was stung on the lip and has since merely watched the bees flying by without trying to catch them. Cat owned by Diane Quaas-Lopez.

behind, however). Should the stinger be on the foot or other part of the body, try to locate and remove it—with care. Swab the area with methylated spirits or apply a suitable antiseptic. Check the wound daily to see that it heals. Should it start to appear septic, you then need to refer this to your vet for treatment.

In the case of snake bites, immobilize the cat, try to keep it calm, and try to identify the species of snake so your vet can use the appropriate serum. Apply a tourniquet above the wound and dab the wound with permanganate crystals if these are readily at hand.

SHOCK AND FITS

If a cat is of a nervous disposition to start with, then it may easily be frightened into a state of shock—even a strong, healthy Burmese could go into shock if a large dog were to grab hold of it in its jaws and shake it. At the moment of the incident, the cat appears just frightened, and its body reacts out of instinctive self-preservation to flee or fight back. However, once the source of the fright has gone, the tremendous energies which the cat has used up in tension and escape start to tell and the cat may collapse. It will lose body heat rapidly as the metabolic systems all try to normalize themselves at the same time; the nervous system cannot cope with all the messages it is passing to the brain and elsewhere, so the result is a temporary "shutdown"—which we term shock.

In such a state, the last thing the cat needs is more stimuli to react to—lights, noises or a hysterical owner! Place the cat in a darkened, quiet room and cover it with a blanket to conserve heat. Normally, the cat will recover in a variable amount of time, depending on the animal and the extent of the shock to its systems. There is little else you can do in such cases, as a vet will be required to assess the full impact of matters, especially where there may be internal hemorrhage, which complicates matters. If the ambient temperature is already warm, then place only a light blanket or sheet over the cat, because too much heat will induce sweating, which will actually increase heat loss.

Fits are treated in the same manner because shock to the nervous system is causal of this complaint. Any saliva coming from the cat's mouth should be gently wiped away. Fits may be recurrent in older cats subject to them, and little can be done other than to provide isolation until the fit passes, usually after a few minutes. The vet will administer injections that may help.

POISON

As with snake bites, it is helpful if the source is known, but often this is not the case, so the first thing to do is to try and get the cat to vomit by giving it an emetic, such as a strong salt solution or bicarbonate of soda. If the cat is only semi-conscious then do not give emetics. Once the system has been cleared of the poison, an antidote is required to neutralize poison absorbed into the stomach wall or the bloodstream. Such chemicals combine with the poison to form harmless chemicals. Antidotes can be used only if the poison is known for certain. Of course the vet should be notified at the same time.

Finally, the patient needs to be treated for shock. Should the poison be one of a corrosive type and which the cat has become covered in, then it should be quickly washed in a soapy detergent to remove the poison.

BURNS

Burns may be caused by corrosives as described under poisons, and should be treated the same, that is, removed by liberal use of soap and water. Burns created by dry heat, such as fire, will be readily seen as the fur will be charred, but scalds produced by liquids may not be noticed for hours or even a day or two. Treatment is the same, however; cover the burnt area with petroleum jelly, after having first applied an ice cold pack to the burn in order to relieve pain. The jelly will prevent bacteria from entering the burn, which

Facing page: Quadruple Grand Champion Chinthe's Microbe. This sable male is owned by Mary DePew.

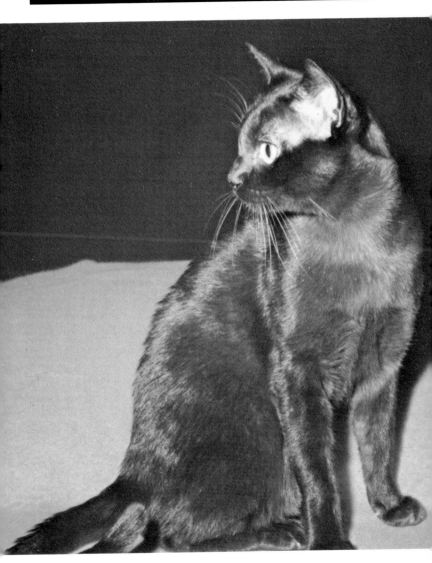

will be sterile of germs. Cover with a clean bandage. In the case of liquid scalds, the first signs may not appear for a while, as the fur will tend to hide the burn. Only the appearance of a swelling, or pus running from it, might indicate that a burn has occurred. Treatment of all but the most minor cases should be referred to a veterinarian, because treatment may be possible only under a local or general anesthetic. Again, shock in its many aspects is normally a side effect

Snakes are sometimes vicious, even though they are not poisonous. This is a *Lampropeltis getulus californiae* with an aberrant color pattern. These snakes are vicious and they bite many cats that grab them or frighten them, but they are not poisonous.

that must be treated.

EAR PROBLEMS

If your cat appears to be scratching its ears a lot, they should be examined to see if grass may have entered the ear; remove it with care and swab with mild antiseptic cream or powder. However, it is more likely that you will see a brown wax-like substance which would indicate ear mites. Use a cotton swab dipped in warm olive oil and wipe away the debris, without probing deep into the ear. If the condition persists, it may be that the cause is either fungal or bacterial, in which case your veterinarian will supply the appropriate treatment for you to use; the vet will also give the ear a thorough cleaning.

RINGWORM

Fungal infection can also produce the sores known as ringworm on the body. These are highly contagious to other pets, or may have come from them. The sores are circular and develop crust-like edges. They can be treated, but such treatment is usually lengthy because the spores are able to live long periods without a host—in blankets, bedding and similar places. These items should be destroyed by burning.

FIRST AID

Cat owners are recommended to purchase any books that include a wide ranging medical section on feline problems and also on first aid. It is always worthwhile to maintain a family first aid box which can be shared with your pets.

Make sure that your family first aid kit contains the necessities for your Burmese, too. Do NOT include flea and tick sprays or anything else which might be poisonous to humans.

Index